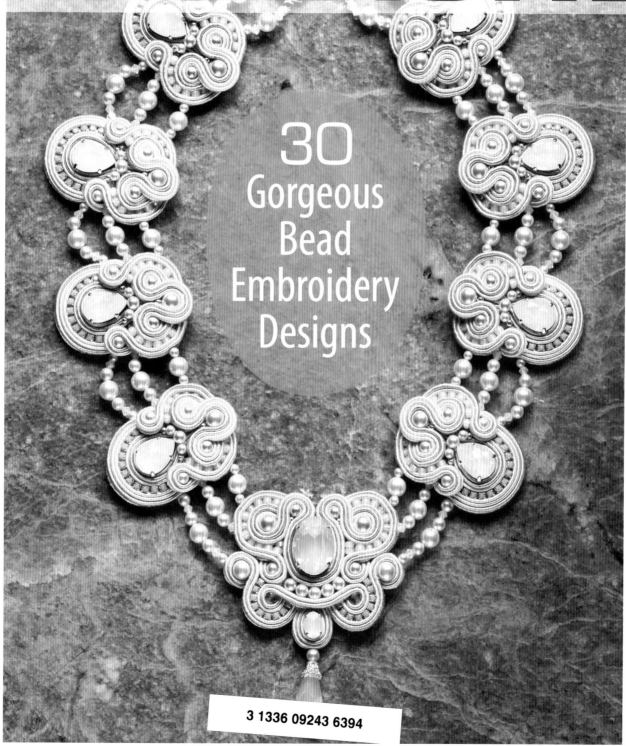

SOUTACHE

30 Gorgeous Bead Embroidery Designs

LARK JEWELRY
& BEADING

Anneta Valious

LARK JEWELRY & BEADING

An Imprint of Sterling Publishing
387 Park Avenue South
New York, NY 10016

ISBN 978-1-4547-0757-8

Distributed in Canada by Sterling Publishing
c/o Canadian Manda Group, 165 Dufferin Street
Toronto, Ontario, Canada M6K 3H6
Distributed in the United Kingdom by GMC Distribution Services
Castle Place, 166 High Street, Lewes, East Sussex, England BN7 1XU
Distributed in Australia by Capricorn Link (Australia) Pty. Ltd.
P.O. Box 704, Windsor, NSW 2756, Australia

For information about custom editions, special sales, and premium and corporate purchases, please
contact Sterling Special Sales at 800-805-5489 or specialsales@sterlingpublishing.com.

Email academic@larkbooks.com for information about desk and examination copies.
The complete policy can be found at larkbooks.com.

Every effort has been made to ensure that all the information in this book is accurate. However,
due to differing conditions, tools, and individual skills, the publisher cannot be responsible for any
injuries, losses, and other damages that may result from the use of the information in this book.

Manufactured in China

2 4 6 8 10 9 7 5 3 1

larkbooks.com

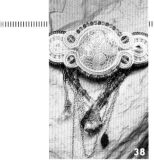

CONTENTS

EXTRAVAGANT PROJECTS FEATURING CRYSTALS

SOUTACHE THROUGH TIME

1. *Portrait of Yevgraf Davidov*
by Orest Kiprensky, 1809
http://en.wikipedia.org/wiki/File:Kiprensky_Davydov.jpg,
collection of the Russian Museum

2. Reproduction of an 1862 Confederate general's
kepi from the American Civil War
Photo courtesy of Andy Fulks, Fall Creek Corporation

3. Members of the modern-day Gardehusarregi-
mentet cavalry unit in Denmark
Photo by Nathalie Mornu

THE MATERIAL I USE TO MAKE JEWELRY may seem new to you, but it's been around for a long time. These days, if people even recognize the word *soutache*, they generally think of it as merely a trim for lampshades, as the material used to make the Chinese fastenings called frogs, and as the stuff of macramé and fancy braidwork. Home sewers sometimes use soutache to add a touch of romance to their projects—that includes garments, and that's where we return to its roots.

Soutache embroidery first developed in France in the fifteenth century, when trim was applied to dresses and coats, and it was also used in the fabrication of jewelry. At that point, soutache was reserved for the aristocracy. By the seventeenth and eighteenth centuries—if history was never your strong suit, just imagine Marie Antoinette and you're in the ballpark!—soutache had become an essential element of the elaborate, frilly attire of the royal court, taking its place alongside ribbon, lace, edgings, and other ornate trimmings and passe-menterie. Of course, France was very influential, so its styles spread across Europe and elsewhere.

In the early 1800s, under Napoleon, braid became prominent on military uniforms. The hussars, a cavalry regiment that originated in Hungary, wore perhaps the most celebrated and some of the most splendid of uniforms, with designs of gold, white, or red soutache. It's no coincidence that the hussars had a reputation for conquering the hearts of many a woman—the dashing uniform certainly had something to do with it! In the United States, too, soutache had its place. Look at Civil War photos and you'll see soldiers holding hats with soutache designs.

Throughout Europe and North America, soutache was omnipresent on administrative and police uniforms, as well. Today still, you'll find bits of soutache on military uniforms to reveal rank or embellish a peaked cap. The beauty of the uniforms of the royal guards of Belgium, Denmark, England, and Morocco, blanketed as they are in soutache embroidery, explains part of their enduring appeal for tourists.

With the dawn of the Industrial Revolution and mechanization, inexpensive ribbon and braid meant that dresses could be embellished more cheaply. Furthermore, the widespread availability of cotton fabric (due to the colonization of the Americas) had a democratizing effect on fashion. Affordable clothing—beautified with soutache—became a staple of department stores. From its inception, soutache embroidery evolved in many ways across the globe, and it's especially interesting to study the different, subtle ways the trim was applied to traditional garb in Eastern Europe.

By the mid-nineteenth century, dress for women and children became simpler, less ornamented. Girls wore plain dresses decorated with little more than a single band of soutache, gimp, or lace. During the period of 1870 to 1890, however, the silhouette changed radically, with skirts and jackets very much festooned with ornamentation. Soutache embroidery regained popularity; it takes center stage on a Victorian coat of the era featuring a design of peacock feathers that's particularly magnificent on the skirt and sleeves.

The clothing styles that followed in the twentieth century simplified radically, and the widespread use of soutache faded, but it made little comebacks from time to time—adding a bit of frivolity to flapper dresses, rendering the swimsuits of bathing beauties of the 1950s utterly impractical, or lending glamour to cocktail gowns.

Soutache embroidery has long been popular as an embellishment on cos-

1

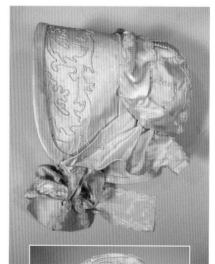

2

3

1. Linen summer dresses embellished with soutache, circa 1865
Collection of Galliera, Museum of the city of Paris fashion
© Stéphane Piera / Galliera / Roger-Viollet / The Image Works

2. Wedding bonnet, circa 1845; soutache on satin and brocade
Photos courtesy of www.antiquedress.com

3. Dress for a boy or girl, circa 1865
Brooklyn Museum Costume Collection at The Metropolitan Museum
of Art, Gift of the Brooklyn Museum, 2009; Gift of the Jason and Peggy
Westerfield Collection, 1969; Accession Number 2009.300.930

4. Dress, circa 1910
Photos courtesy of www.antiquedress.com

5. Victorian coat, circa 1890; soutache on wool
Photos courtesy of www.antiquedress.com

6. Bodice of a Richilene cocktail dress from the 1970s
Photo by Maggie Muellner

7. Tabard dress from the 1920s
Photos by Margaret Davidson, www.pennydreadfulvintage.com

tumes for the stage, but also in other kinds of spectacle. It plays its own part as marching bands perform and contributes to the richness of the suit of lights donned by Spanish bullfighters. Couture designers constantly reinvent their collections with the help of fancy trims, edgings, and such. Military uniforms frequently serve as inspiration for modern fashion. Models strut the catwalks of Chanel and Dolce & Gabbana in tweed jackets trimmed with piping, braid, and soutache. And on the red carpet, the stars pose, resplendent in fabulous frocks enhanced with organza flowers and swirls of soutache.

Recent times have seen a renewed interest in adornments embroidered from beads and soutache, particularly jewelry. The technique has become especially popular in France, Poland, other European countries, and Israel. Artists appreciate the wide variety of applications soutache has on stunning necklaces, bracelets, earrings, and brooches.

Now, with the instructions in this book, you can make your own beautiful and elegant soutache creations. Join me on this fun creative adventure!

1. A bullfighter
© iStockphoto/Syldavia

2. Marching band
© iStockphoto/Cascoly

3. From the runway of the Dolce & Gabbana men's winter 2009/2010 collection
© IMAXtree.com/Alessandro Lucioni

4. Actress Lisa Edelstein at the 2008 Emmy awards
© Frazer Harrison/Getty Images

MATERIALS AND TOOLS

One of the many wonderful things about soutache jewelry is that the materials and tools you need are very few. Here's an introduction to all the items you need to create your own pieces.

Materials

When you shop for materials, *get the best quality you can afford*. I can't stress this enough. Soutache jewelry looks lush and elegant—but only if you don't skimp.

Soutache

Soutache is a French word derived from the Hungarian *sujtás*. This flat braid has a groove down its center and comes in a wide range of colors, ranging from 3/32 to 5/16 inch (2 to 8 mm) wide. It's made of two rows of piping or cording wrapped in viscose (rayon), cotton, or synthetic fibers, depending on the manufacturer. To determine the quality of a given soutache, the only method is to handle it. Superior soutache is fairly thick along the edge—the part you'll see in the finished project—and the wrapping should be smooth with no pulled threads. Note that some companies produce a "pseudo-soutache" from just a braid. Don't use that type, as it's very hard to work with. Make sure the soutache you buy is made the traditional way with a base of cording.

For making jewelry, select soutache that's 1/8 inch (3 mm) wide. Ideally, the base piping should be the same color as the exterior fibers.

> For the sake of diversity, I use the terms *trim*, *braid*, and *soutache* interchangeably.

Cabochons and Pendants

With a flat bottom and a rounded top, cabochons may be made from gemstones, glass, metal, wood, resin, or a host of other materials. Cabs, as they're often called, dictate the shape and style of a piece of jewelry made with soutache. You'll frequently use them as the focal element of a design. They don't only have to be round or oval. You'll find cabs that are rectangular or even irregular in shape.

Pendants with a predrilled hole can also be used for soutache jewelry, as long as they have a flat back like a cabochon. You can disguise the holes by embellishing them with beads; I've used pendants in several projects in this book.

Crystal Stones

Crystal stones lend luxury and sparkle to soutache jewelry. You'll find them in many shades, shapes, and styles, including foil-backed rivolis and faceted octagons, ovals, and pears. Several projects call for stones that are mounted in prong settings. These are available commercially as a unit, but you can also mount individual stones quite easily in prong settings bought separately (see page 21 for more information). You may also use seed beads to weave a bezel for a crystal stone in a project or two. This is explained on page 24.

If you can't locate a stone that's exactly the same size as the one I used in a project, get one that's as near as possible to it, and adjust the quantity of soutache you use. Especially if your stone is larger, you'll want to make sure you have extra soutache on hand just in case.

In case you want to exactly replicate the projects in this book, I've created a list that tells you precisely which crystal stones and crystal beads I've used, and in what colors. You can find it on my publisher's website at www.larkcrafts.com/bonus, or on my website at www.annetavalious.com.

Beads

All sorts of beads, whether made from glass, metal, or precious stones, are perfect for soutache jewelry. You can use round beads, bicones, drops, rondelles, and anything else you happen to have in your stash. These are for creating the bands, fringes, and embellishments that make a piece of jewelry unique. Most of the beads I use measure 4 to 6 mm.

For visual weight and additional color, I add seed beads to my designs. These also serve to hide the spaces between the rows of soutache and to give the work a finished appearance. Select high-quality seed beads. Any flaws and differences in size in the beads will be glaringly visible, maybe more so than in bead embroidery and bead-weaving. The sizes of seed beads are given as a numeral preceding either "/0" or "°," which is pronounced *ott*. I use mostly 11° and 8° seed beads.

Rhinestone Chain

Rhinestone chain adds a particularly charming touch when combined into soutache jewelry. You can sew it around cabochons or between layers of soutache trim. Manufacturers make it in different colors of glass and assorted widths, with the option of silver, gold, or bronze metal finishes that you can match to your other materials. I use rhinestone chain measuring 1.5 to 3 mm across because I think it looks the most refined.

Feathers

Add drama to your pieces by including feathers. (You'll catch the ends between the back of the beadwork and the backing.) Craft stores sell a few types of feathers, but for a more abundant selection, search online. You can get them dyed or natural. If they're attached to a strip of fabric, you can simply snip them off it. Here's just a sampling of the many varieties available.

- Goose feathers are probably offered in every craft store.

- Coque tail feathers are narrow, with downy bottoms and stiff barbs along the rest of the quill.

- Duck flank feathers are soft and spotted.

- Emu and ostrich—think boas. The feathers are long, skinny, and fluttery.

- Goose biots are spiky and stiff, with an almost oily appearance. You can curl them.

- Stripped rooster hackles consist of a bare shaft tipped with some fluff. If you like this look but can't find any, just strip the barbs off the bottom of whatever feathers you do have.

Findings

There are many types of findings available in a variety of metals and finishes. For the projects in this book, you'll need clasps for necklaces and bracelets, backings for brooches and barrettes, shanks for rings, jump rings, ear wires, fold-over ends, and so on. (For earrings you can use hooks, studs, or clip-ons based on your preference.) You'll also use metal rings and chain. Each set of project instructions will list exactly which findings you need to complete the piece of jewelry.

Buy only high-quality findings. You'll be terribly disappointed if, after all your careful beading, a metal finding starts to oxidize or change color. I recommend you avoid using findings and beads made of sterling silver in a project if they're going to touch the braid itself. Remember that soutache jewelry is made from a textile. Silver tarnishes and might stain the trim as it does so.

You can wear soutache pendants dangling from purchased neck rings or from chain. And you might like the effect of hanging them from velvet ribbon or strips of silk, or any other fancy material you find attractive.

Base and Backing Material

Some of the projects will require a fabric base; you'll glue cabochons onto it. The fabric should be rigid and fairly thick, and it should resist fraying. I use synthetic suede in colors matching the cab or the soutache, and also use a specialized beading foundation called Lacy's Stiff Stuff.

To cover the embroidery and give the work a nice, tidy finish, you'll make a backing of lightweight material. You can use any of the following:

- leather, 1/64 to 1/32 inch (0.5 to 0.7 mm) thick
- synthetic leather
- suede
- synthetic suede

Synthetic suede is the easiest to work with. Because it's soft, it will feel nice against your skin when used on necklaces and bracelets. Leather, on the other hand, gives a professional finish and you can clean it with a gentle hand soap or leather cleaner.

In a few projects, I tell you to place a transparent plastic film between the embroidery and the lining to stiffen the embroidery work. In its place, you can also use thin, flexible plastic or cardstock.

Other projects call for polyester stuffing to fill in the empty spaces on the back of the work, between the ends of soutache. Adding this filler material provides padding that's especially nice for bracelets.

Thread

For soutache jewelry, a strong, fine thread is best. The nylon threads commonly used in beadweaving work perfectly. Keep the essential colors on hand—gray, beige, off-white, and black—but eventually, you'll want to have a complete palette of shades.

Choose your thread color carefully. It needs to be the same shade as the soutache visible on the edge of the jewelry. For pieces that contain more than one hue of soutache, you might have to use different colors of thread. You'd use white thread to stitch pale soutache on a multicolored piece of jewelry, for example, and black thread to sew the areas made from dark soutache.

Thread color is also based on the type of beads you're using. Remember that dark thread will show through transparent beads—but that may be the desired outcome! Finally, avoid transparent polyethylene thread; it will reflect bright light (like the sun) and become quite visible.

Adhesive

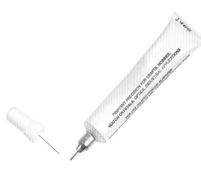

You'll need some kind of glue to finish the ends of the soutache. I generally use a cement specifically designed for jewelry repair sold in a tube that has an applicator tip. The tip allows me to control both the amount and the placement of the glue. You'll also use an adhesive to adhere cabochons and other focal elements to the base fabric. For this, go with anything you like. Any industrial-strength adhesive will work, as does cyanoacrylate. What's important is to select an adhesive compatible with whatever material you plan to attach, whether glass, wood, or gemstones. *Note:* Some stones—turquoise and amber in particular—may be damaged by strong adhesives. Be sure to read the manufacturer's instructions carefully.

Tools

Making soutache jewelry requires next to no tools.

Beading Needles

You need long, fine needles, the same kind you'd use for beadweaving. Keep at least two sizes on hand. Use size 10 for sewing the soutache, attaching the lining, and adding embellishments. Use size 12 for working with seed beads. Because it's a smaller needle, you'll be able to pass through the beads several times as needed.

Scissors

Small scissors with extremely sharp, fine tips will make your work easier and cause the finished piece to look much cleaner. Embroidery or manicure scissors are ideally suited to soutache embroidery. You can use them to cut anything that's not metal.

Pliers and Wire Cutters

Get two pairs of chain-nose pliers for working with jump rings, which you'll use for attaching clasps and other findings to the embroidered elements. Wire cutters are useful for cutting rhinestone chain as well as chain.

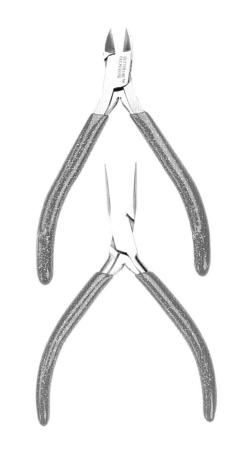

Thread Burner

This little gizmo is optional. If you feel comfortable with one of these, you can use it to finish the ends of synthetic soutache rather than coating them in glue (page 15). Note that only synthetic soutache can be finished in this way, because natural fibers won't melt.

A thread burner has a tip that gets hot enough to melt the synthetic threads. Simply press a button on the side, hold the tip to the trim you want to melt and secure, and then remove the tool once the threads curl up. Allow the area to cool for a few seconds before touching it.

You can use a lighter or a match instead, but you won't have the kind of precision you do with a thread burner.

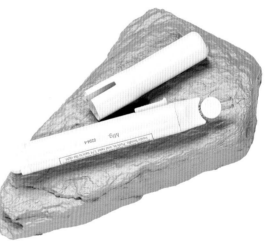

Tracing Paper and Pencil

To make the backing for your soutache jewelry, you'll trace the various elements and make a pattern. Any type of lightweight paper and a regular pencil will be just fine for this step.

Tape Measure

You'll need to measure pieces of braid, the circumference of the wrist to determine the lengths of bracelets, and other things. It's handier to do with a tape measure than with a rigid ruler.

TECHNIQUES

Read through this section to learn about the methods I use in my work. Pay special attention to the boxes scattered throughout; they contain essential information that you should keep in mind as you make your own soutache projects.

THE ESSENTIALS

Unless I tell you differently, stitch using the entire length of trim you have left on hand. Why?

- The ends will fray a bit and become unusable, so you waste some material each time you cut additional pieces.

- Longer pieces are easier to handle, so you can keep better tension as you sew.

- It takes a lot of experience to estimate exactly how much soutache you'll need to make a given element of embroidery.

Sometimes you do need to cut a piece to a specific length, and the instructions will tell you to do so. If you're adding additional layers of soutache to an element you've already constructed, you can cut them to the length of the initial layer.

Stitching

The quality of your hand stitching makes all the difference. It's essential to sew with small, regular stitches, which requires patience and care. Stick your needle precisely through the groove in the trim, making sure you don't hook or pull any of the threads that are part of the soutache. A sharp needle helps in this process, and using thread that matches the color of the braid will help keep your stitches invisible.

With a little practice, you'll pull off perfect stitches in no time! Here's how.

1 Thread your needle with a comfortable length of thread and knot one end. (In other words, don't work with the thread doubled.) The knot will be hidden either on the back of the work or between the layers of soutache.

2 To practice, cut two or three pieces of soutache of say, oh, 8 inches (20.3 cm). Arrange the pieces of soutache so they face the same direction. Tack them together with a few stitches, hiding the knot between the layers of trim.

THE LONG AND THE SHORT OF IT

How much thread should you use? Different beaders feel comfortable sewing with different lengths. I'm comfortable with roughly 24 to 32 inches (61 to 81.3 cm). It's really up to you. You don't want so much that it snarls up. Yet you don't want to waste a lot of time threading your needle because you're working with hardly any thread at all. Try to determine how much you'll need for a given seam and cut a little more than that.

---

3 Bring your needle out of the trim exactly in the groove.

4 Stick the needle precisely back in the same spot, and pass it through all the layers of soutache at a slight angle so it exits the last piece of trim exactly in the groove (photo 1). Keep working on this technique until you achieve invisible stitches (photo 2).

Any imperfection will remain visible in a piece of finished jewelry. If your stitching looks bad—which can happen to anyone, but especially a beginner—it's really best to gently rip it out and start over.

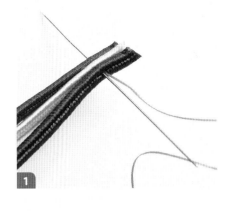

> ### THE ESSENTIALS
> - As you sew a project, keep using the same thread until you run out or until it no longer matches the color of the soutache or beads. If the thread color doesn't match the rest of the work it will be noticeable.
> - When the thread becomes too short to work with, or when you finish a seam, just draw your needle to the back of the work. Don't make a knot. Instead, fasten off the thread by making a few tight parallel stitches, concealing them as much as possible. Dab a drop of glue on the spot to secure it.

Finishing the Ends of Soutache

The ends of the trim have a tendency to fray. After you've finished a seam, don't just cut the soutache willy-nilly! Instead, give the work a tidy appearance by either treating the ends with glue, or melting and securing them together with a thread burner. (I prefer using glue.)

Most of the time, the instructions will tell you to fold the soutache to the back of the work to hide the ends, so of course you'll need to leave enough extra trim to turn to the back.

1 Soak the soutache with glue at the spot you want to cut (photo 3).

2 As soon as it starts to dry, trim the ends to get a clean, precise cut (photo 4).

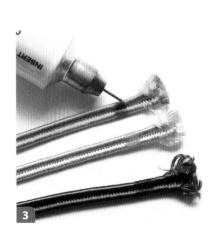

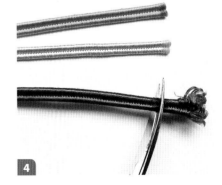

> ### THE ESSENTIALS
> For most of the projects, the method for finishing the ends of the soutache will always be the same:
>
> 1 Fold the ends to the back of the work.
>
> 2 Secure them with a few stitches.
>
> 3 Then apply glue where you want to trim.
>
> 4 Finally, cut off any excess soutache.
>
> The process is slightly different for small pieces of beadwork, such as earrings. In that case, begin by folding back the ends of the soutache but do not stitch them down yet. Figure out where you'll need to cut, apply the glue to that spot, and then trim away any extra material. Finally, stitch down the ends on the back of the beadwork.

Attaching Soutache around a Bead

You're going to incorporate beads in just about every piece of soutache jewelry. For this particular technique, it doesn't matter what shape they are because the method will be the same. When you're just learning to work with soutache, begin by surrounding the beads with one row of trim at a time; as your technique improves, you may be able to stitch multiple layers simultaneously. But please only one row to begin!

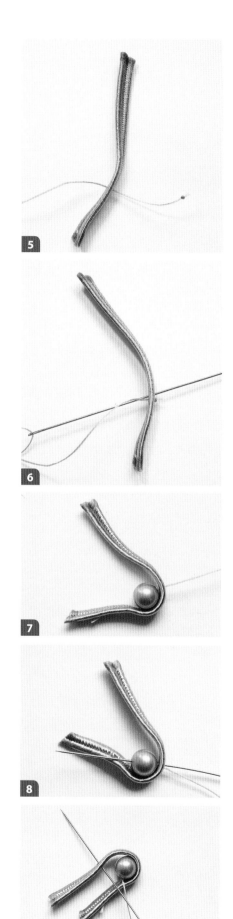

> **THE ESSENTIALS**
> Each time you begin to stitch using the entire length of soutache, leave 2 inches (5.1 cm) of unattached allowance unless the instructions tell you differently. When you're working with shorter lengths cut to a precise measurement, always leave at least 1 inch (2.5 cm) of unattached allowance.

1 Begin by securing the knot in the soutache; the tiny knots can pull through the trim, so be sure to block your knot with a first stitch as follows: Insert the needle through the trim from the outside (photo 5), stitch back through from the inside (photo 6), and complete the blocking stitch by inserting the needle back from the outside once again. This first little stitch keeps the knot in place—don't forget it!

2 With the thread coming out of the groove in the soutache, string on a bead, wrap the trim around it, and poke your needle through the trim (photo 7).

3 Stick your needle back through the bead, poking it close to the spot from which the thread is exiting (photo 8).

4 Wrap the soutache completely around the bead and poke the needle through where the trim meets the hole in the bead (photo 9).

5 Sew both layers of soutache together below the bead, making several stitches (photo 10).

Now you can add one or more additional rows of soutache. As you do, be careful to always stitch through the groove in the trim (photo 11). After stitching all the way around, tack the layers of soutache together at the base of the bead with a few stitches (photo 12).

> **THE ESSENTIALS**
> When you're attaching beads, remember these two things:
>
> • Always make an initial blocking stitch to secure the knot.
>
> • Always surround beads with one row of soutache at a time until you've mastered the technique.

When you stitch a row of beads to an element that already exists, always have the needle come out of the back of the work, stitching through as many of the existing layers as possible. Your stitches will be hidden by the backing.

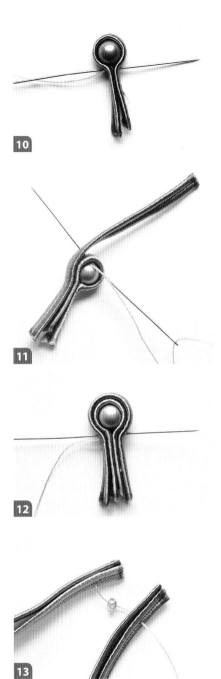

10

11

12

13

Making Bands

Nestle beads between borders of soutache to create simple strips, and use them to fasten on necklaces and bracelets, or for other parts of jewelry. In general, beads 4 to 7 mm in diameter work best for this purpose. Beads smaller than that will be hard to see between the rows of trim, while larger beads are difficult to work with.

You can use as many rows of soutache as you'd like, but if you're just starting, I'd suggest using only two or three layers.

First, determine how much soutache you need, using the following formula. Decide how long of a finished strip you want. Calculate 30 percent of that measurement. Add the 30 percent to the original length—that's how long each strip of soutache needs to be. (Don't get bogged down in exact calculations; just round off.)

Say, for example, you want a strip 15 inches (38.1 cm) long. Thirty percent of that is 5 inches (12.7 cm). Add the two numbers together and you get 20 inches (50.8 cm). *Note:* If you plan to make a band in which the piece of soutache will be folded in half, double the amount of soutache you start with.

Bands with a Row of Seed Beads

In many projects, you'll add a row of seed beads around a larger bead or cabochon you've already stitched down. However, you may create a row of seed beads that's completely independent of any other beads. If you're working with soutache that's ⅛ inch (3 mm) wide, 8° seed beads are the ideal size to use.

1 Tack two pieces of soutache together near the ends. String on a seed bead.

2 Poke your needle through two additional pieces of soutache (photo 13).

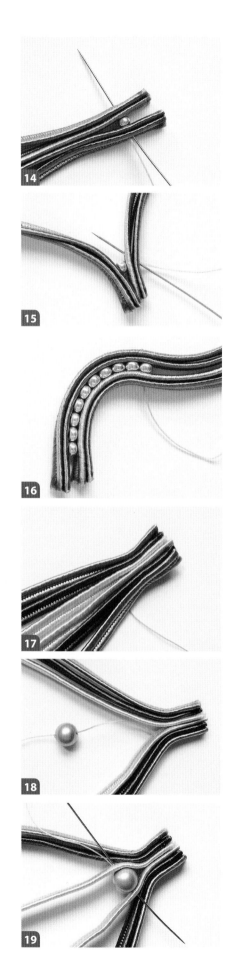

3 Insert the needle close to the spot from which the thread is coming out, then go back through all the layers of soutache and the seed bead. This way, the bead will be held in place securely (photo 14).

4 Insert the needle back through both layers of soutache, ¹⁄₁₆ to ⅛ inch (1.5 to 2 mm) from the seed bead (photo 15). String on another seed bead and stitch it in place as described in step 3. Keep adding more seed beads in the same fashion until you've got as many as you like in the row. Pay special attention to the spacing between the seed beads—it should be even. Don't crowd the beads, but don't leave wide spaces between them, either.

You can make a band straight or shape it with a curve, depending on the design of the jewelry.

Making Curves

Even though this doesn't seem like it should work, trust me on it. To make curves, simply hold two pieces of soutache exactly in the shape you want to achieve and stitch them together. Because the inner curve of material is shorter than the outer curve, the stitches hold everything immobile (photo 16).

Bands Using Round or Flat Beads

You can also make bands with larger beads, but you'll tack the layers of soutache together between each bead. As with seed beads, the holes in the beads are perpendicular to the rows of soutache surrounding them.

1 Cut six pieces of soutache all the same length; vary the colors as appropriate. With all the pieces facing the same way, make a few stitches near the end to hold them together (photo 17). Divide the soutache into two groups of three each.

2 Bring your needle out of a groove so it's between both groups. String on a bead (photo 18).

3 Sew the bead between the two innermost rows of soutache to hold it in place (photo 19), stitching back and forth a time or two. Then sew through all the outer layers (photo 20) to tack them together, passing the needle back and forth through the bead to secure both sides.

4 Pass the needle back through the outermost layers of soutache. Sew together the two innermost pieces of soutache just beyond the bead (photo 21). Make several stitches to really secure it. Sew all the layers of soutache together beyond the bead (photo 22).

Repeat steps 2 through 4 until the band is the desired length (photos 23 to 26).

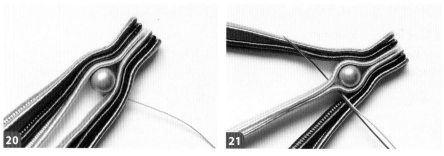

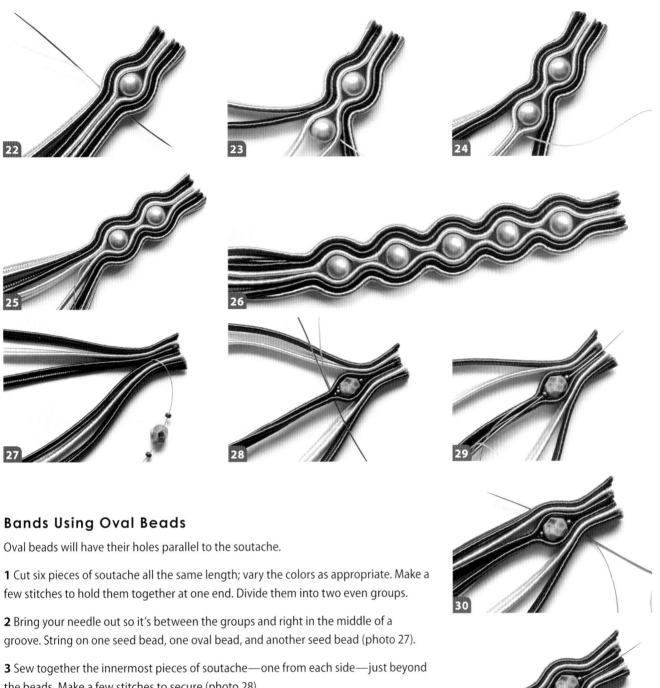

Bands Using Oval Beads

Oval beads will have their holes parallel to the soutache.

1 Cut six pieces of soutache all the same length; vary the colors as appropriate. Make a few stitches to hold them together at one end. Divide them into two even groups.

2 Bring your needle out so it's between the groups and right in the middle of a groove. String on one seed bead, one oval bead, and another seed bead (photo 27).

3 Sew together the innermost pieces of soutache—one from each side—just beyond the beads. Make a few stitches to secure (photo 28).

4 With the needle exiting between the two groups of soutache, pass your needle back through the three beads (photo 29).

5 Sew the pieces of soutache on one side of the beads together, keeping your stitches small and invisible. Finish with the needle exiting the back of the work (photo 30).

6 After the rows of soutache on one side have been sewn, once again position your needle so it exits between the two groups of soutache. Pass the needle through the beads again (photo 31).

7 Now sew together the pieces of soutache on the other side of the bead (photo 32).

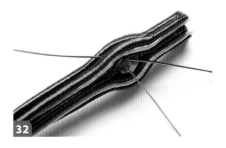

8 Sew all the rows of soutache together beyond the beads (photo 33).

Repeat steps 2 through 8 until your band is the desired length (photos 34 through 37).

Attaching Soutache to a Cabochon

Soutache and cabochons combine to spectacular effect! You can also attach pendants in this manner.

1 Cement the flat bottom of the cabochon to a piece of fray-resistant base fabric, such as synthetic suede or beading foundation.

2 After the adhesive has dried, trim away the base material, leaving ⅛ inch (2 mm) all around the cab.

3 Thread your needle, then pass it through the back of the base fabric so it comes up right next to the cab. Jab the needle right into the groove of the piece of soutache you wish to attach. (Remember that you generally leave a 2-inch [5.1 cm] tail on the trim, as shown in photo 38.)

4 Bring the needle through the soutache and the base fabric, close to the cab, making the stitch ¹⁄₁₆ to ⅛ inch (1.5 to 2 mm) long (photo 39).

5 Continue attaching the soutache all around the cabochon in the manner, making sure the trim rests firmly against the edge of the cab (photo 40). Once you've worked all the way around, attach the two layers of soutache to one another with a few additional stitches (photo 41).

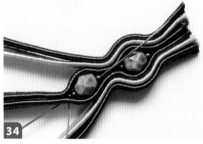

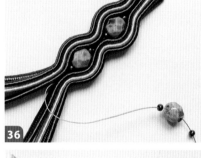

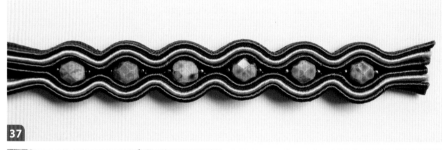

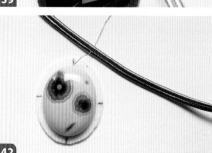

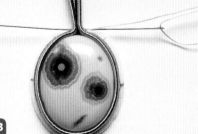

At this point, you can attach more rows of braid, or any other embellishments you like.

If the cabochon is round or oval, mark the axes of symmetry (or cardinal points) on the base material so you have a starting point. Begin attaching the soutache at one of these points; end here as well (photos 42 and 43).

Attaching Soutache to a Prong Setting

A number of the projects in this book contain stones mounted in a prong setting. Make sure that the setting you buy has holes that will allow the needle to pass through so you can stitch soutache to it. You can buy preset units, or stones and prong settings sold separately; see below for instructions on setting them. Another technique for attaching a loose stone or crystal to jewelry is to make a bezel setting for it out of seed beads; you can read about that method on page 24.

1 Make a knot and secure the thread exactly in the groove of the piece of soutache. Pass the needle through two holes in the setting (photo 44).

2 Pass the needle through the soutache. Make sure the trim lies snug against the prong setting. Adjust the soutache around the setting while passing the needle back through the holes (photo 45).

3 Work around the stone as in steps 1 and 2 and then sew the layers of soutache together, lining them up either with one of the prongs or with the middle of one side of the stone, depending on the style of the setting (photo 46).

4 Sew one or more other pieces of soutache to the first one, with the needle coming out behind the crystal to avoid damaging its surface (photo 47).

5 Finish by tacking together all the layers of the soutache with a few tiny stitches (photo 48).

Securing Crystals in Prong Settings

Sometimes prong settings and the stones to fit inside them are sold separately. Mounting the crystal permanently is simple. The only tool you'll need is a pair of flat-nose pliers.

1 Orient the stone correctly in the prong setting and hold it perfectly level during the entire process.

2 Bend over any one prong just slightly. Then bend over the one across from it just a little. Continue in this manner until you've partially bent all of the prongs over.

3 With the stone now held immobile, bend all of the prongs completely over.

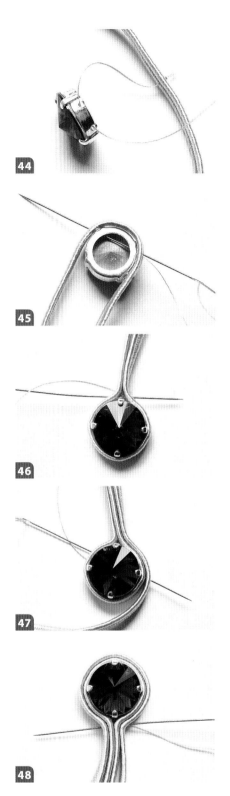

44

45

46

47

48

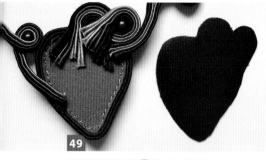

49

50

51

52

53

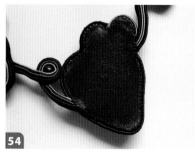

54

Backing the Beadwork

You should finish the back of a piece of jewelry as carefully as you created the front. The appearance of the reverse side is indicative of the overall quality of your workmanship.

1 Place the embroidery face up on a sheet of paper and trace around it.

2 Cut out the shape, place it against the back of the embroidery, and make any necessary adjustments to the pattern.

3 Trace the paper pattern onto a piece of backing material and cut it out (photo 49).

Brooches and pendants will look more professional if you add a layer of stiffener between the beadwork and the lining. To do this, use the same pattern to cut a piece of thin plastic or cardstock. Trim away 1/8 inch (2 mm) from all edges of the plastic or cardstock, and glue it to the wrong side of the backing (photo 50). *Note:* Don't stiffen bracelets or necklaces that graze the collarbone. These types of jewelry should stay soft and supple.

If the back of the beadwork is lumpy, fill any shallow depressions with stuffing (photo 51).

You're now ready to stitch the backing to the bead embroidery.

1 Make a knot in the thread and secure it to the back of the beadwork.

2 Pass the needle under the outermost row of soutache and exit from the groove on the edge of the piece. Place the backing in position.

3 Insert the needle at the same spot it exits the soutache and catch the backing ⅛ inch (2 mm) from the edge. Stitch back through the trim, coming out through the groove. Pull the thread. The edge of the backing will bury itself under the final row of soutache as you stitch. Make every stitch 1/16 to ⅛ inch (1.5 to 2 mm) from the edge of the lining and from the preceding stitch (photos 52 and 53).

4 Keep stitching all around to attach the backing to the beadwork.

5 When you finish, poke the needle between the backing and the soutache. Pull the thread through, but not all the way! Apply a smidge of glue to the thread, close to the backing. Now pull the thread through. The glue will help secure the thread where it's hidden under the backing. Repeat this process several times before cutting the thread (photo 54).

Attaching Fold-Over End Findings

In many cases, the clasps for holding on necklaces, pendants, and bracelets can be attached simply by running one or more pieces of soutache through a ring that's part of the mechanism. But some of the projects call for fold-over end findings. This bent metal finding has something like a jaw with little teeth along one edge for securing ribbon and (what else?) soutache. Along the fold is a loop to which you'll connect your clasp.

1 Apply glue to the ends of the soutache you want to attach inside the fold-over end finding and cut them straight (photo 55).

55

2 Gather the pieces of soutache together, making sure they all face the same way. Stitch the ends together to make sure they'll stay put when you place them in the end finding.

3 Place the ends of the soutache into the jaw of the end finding. Gently squeeze the finding with pliers (photo 56). **Note:** To avoid marring the surface of the fold-over end finding, use pliers with a protective rubber coating or protect the finding with some fabric.

56

Hiding Holes in Pendants or Focal Beads

You can use any flat-backed bead as a focal element, even if it has a hole drilled in it. Think of it as another opportunity to embellish while you hide the hole! You'll be working on a focal bead that's been glued to a foundation.

To hide the hole, use either an 11° or an 8° seed bead and work as follows: Pass your needle up through the hole in the pendant or cabochon, working through the foundation from the back of the work to the front. String on the seed bead, then pass your needle back through the hole in the flat-backed bead so that it comes out through the foundation. Secure the thread.

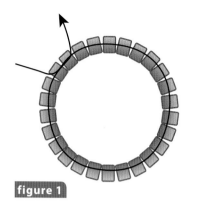

figure 1

Making a Peyote Stitch Bezel around Rivolis

This is the method I use for the projects in this book, using a combination of size 11° Delicas and size 15° seed beads.

1 Thread your needle without cutting the thread off the spool.

2 Pick up the amount of Delicas given in the instructions. Pass through the first two beads strung to make a ring (figure 1).

3 Pick up a Delica, skip a bead, and pass your needle into the next bead. This pattern is called peyote stitch. Repeat, working your way around the ring. You now have three rows of Delicas, because the initial ring of beads splits into rows 1 and 2, and the Delicas added in this step become row 3.

Note: Starting at the end of row 3, and every row thereafter, pass into the first bead of the previous row. This is called a step up.

4 Switch to 15° seed beads. Stitch two rows of peyote stitch (figure 2). As you add each bead, pull on the thread. This will cause the beadwork to cup.

5 Place the rivoli into the half-finished bezel, face up.

6 Weave to the very first row of beads you created. Using strong thread tension, hold the rivoli in place as you peyote stitch two rows of 15° seed beads against the back of the stone, as shown in figure 3. Secure the beadwork by passing your needle through all the beads in the last row of 15° beads again. Don't cut the tails. You can use them later to attach the bezeled rivoli to your soutache embroidery.

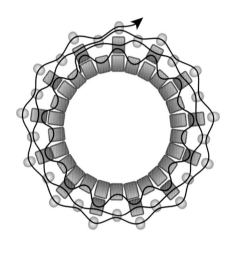

figure 2

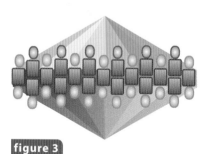

figure 3

VINTAGE BRACELET

Tucked between powdery shades of soutache, freshwater pearls—so popular in classic jewelry—are shown off to their best advantage. The design of this simple bracelet, combined with a carefully chosen clasp, has a refined, retro look.

Gather

1⅛ yards (1 m)* each of soutache in beige, light pink, and rose

20 to 26 freshwater pearls, 8 mm

Size 11° pink seed beads, 1 g

1 gold-colored decorative clasp

2 gold-colored jump rings, 5 mm

1½ x 1½ inches (3.8 x 3.8 cm) of dark pink leather

Tape measure

Beading thread

Industrial-strength glue

Tracing paper

Scissors

Beading needles

2 pairs of flat-nose pliers

Pencil

* See the box below.

Dimensions

1 x 7½ inches (2.5 x 19 cm)

START WITH ENOUGH

When you start stitching this design, each piece of soutache will need to measure at least three times the desired length of the bracelet.

Stitch

1 Leaving a 2 inch-tail (5.1 cm) of thread, sew together the three pieces of soutache (photo a).

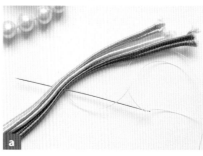

2 String on a pearl and wrap it in the rows of soutache (photo b). Pass the needle back through the rows of soutache and through the pearl to strengthen the stitching and hold the pearl securely in place (photo c).

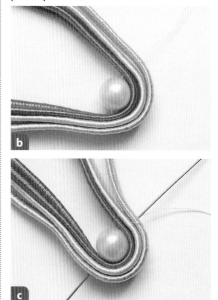

3 Being sure to keep your stitches hidden, sew all the layers of soutache together all around the pearl (photo d).

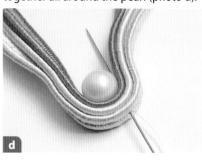

4 String on a seed bead and arrange it below the pearl. Join the six layers of braid (photo e). Sew the rows of soutache together below the bead, making several stitches to hold it securely (photo f). Note how the seed bead fills the gap where the rows of soutache meet.

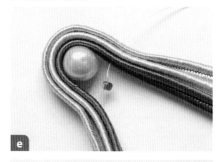

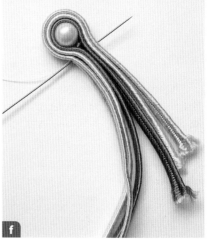

5 Bring the thread out on the side with the long tails of the braid. String on a pearl (photo g).

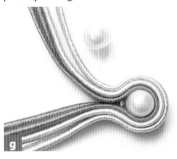

6 Sew the rows of soutache together around the pearl (photo h).

7 Attach a seed bead and sew the six rows of soutache below the bead (photo i).

8 With the thread on the side with the long tails, string on another pearl (photo j). Repeat steps 6 through 8, zigzagging the trim around the pearls, until the piece fits comfortably around your wrist.

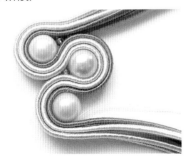

9 Next, attach half of the clasp to one end of the piece as follows. Open a jump ring with two pairs of pliers, hook one part of the clasp on it, then catch the two outer rows of the soutache in it. Close the jump ring (photo k). Sew the soutache around the last pearl on the work. Tuck the ends of the trim to the back of the work (photo l). Attach the other half of the clasp to the other end of the bracelet in the same manner.

10 Apply glue to the ends of the soutache and cut them fairly short. Stitch them to the back of the work.

11 Trace and make a pattern for the ends, cut them out of the leather, and attach them to the wrong side of the beadwork (photo m).

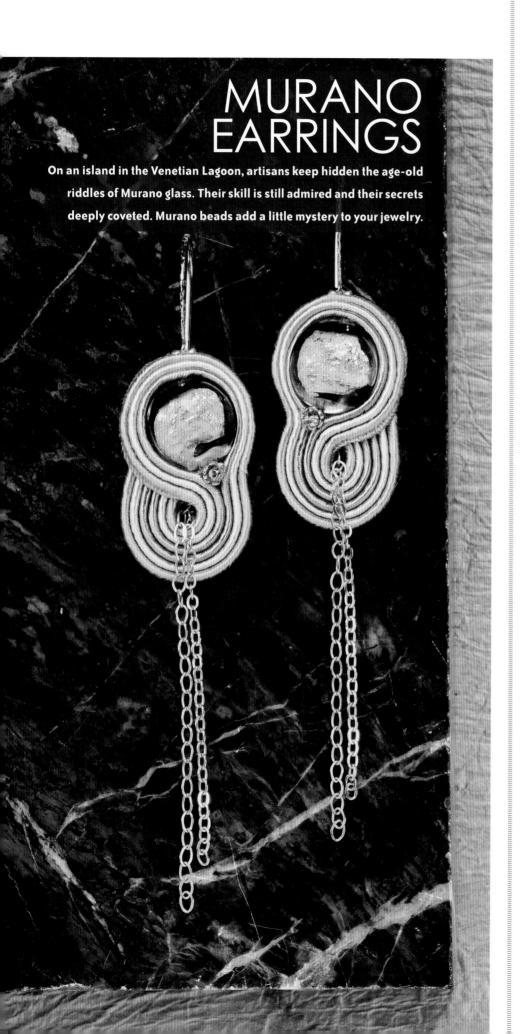

MURANO EARRINGS

On an island in the Venetian Lagoon, artisans keep hidden the age-old riddles of Murano glass. Their skill is still admired and their secrets deeply coveted. Murano beads add a little mystery to your jewelry.

Gather

12 inches (30.5 cm) each of soutache in gray, light gray, and chartreuse

2 flat green lampworked glass beads with gold foil, 14 mm

2 light green 11° seed beads

4 size 15° gold-colored seed beads

2 gold-colored bead caps, 3.5 mm

12 inches (30.5 cm) of gold-colored chain*

2 gold-colored ear wires

2 x 2 inches (5.1 x 5.1 cm) of light green suede

Beading thread

Industrial-strength glue

Tracing paper

Scissors

Beading needles

Tape measure

Pencil

Wire cutters

* For a more eclectic look, get two types of chain of different size, each 7 inches (17.8 cm) long.

Dimensions

1 x 1½ inches (2.5 x 3.8 cm), excluding chain drop

Stitch

Note: You may find it easier to match both earrings by stitching them at the same time, rather than completing one and then starting the next. Do remember to make them as mirror images of each other.

1 Knot the thread and make your first stitch at the midpoint of the trim. String on a glass bead and wrap the piece of gray soutache around it. Join the ends with a few stitches (photo a).

2 Attach the light gray and chartreuse trim, keeping your stitches tiny and invisible, and in the groove of the soutache (photo b).

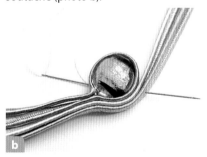

3 Sew all six layers of soutache together where they join (photo c).

4 Bring the thread out below the bead, between the innermost rows of soutache. String on a bead cap and an 11° seed bead (photo d).

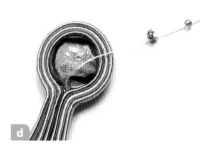

5 Take the needle back through the bead cap and pull the thread tight (photo e). This hides the gap below the focal bead where the rows of soutache meet.

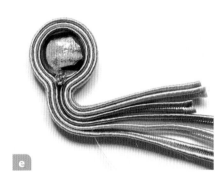

6 Stitch all six layers of soutache together with tiny, invisible stitches, forming them into a curve as you do so. Loop them behind the focal bead, apply glue to the ends, cut them, and stitch them securely to the back of the work (photo f).

7 Cut the chain into four pieces, with two that measure 2¾ inches (7 cm) and two that measure 3⅛ inches (8 cm).

8 Pass one short piece and one long piece of chain through the space inside the curve. Sew the ends to the back of the earring, as shown in photo g.

9 Position an ear wire at the top of the bead embroidery and stitch it to the row of chartreuse trim. Attach a 15° seed bead directly on each side of the ear wire.

10 Trace and make a pattern for the backings, cut them out of the suede, and sew them to the wrong side of the beadwork (photo h).

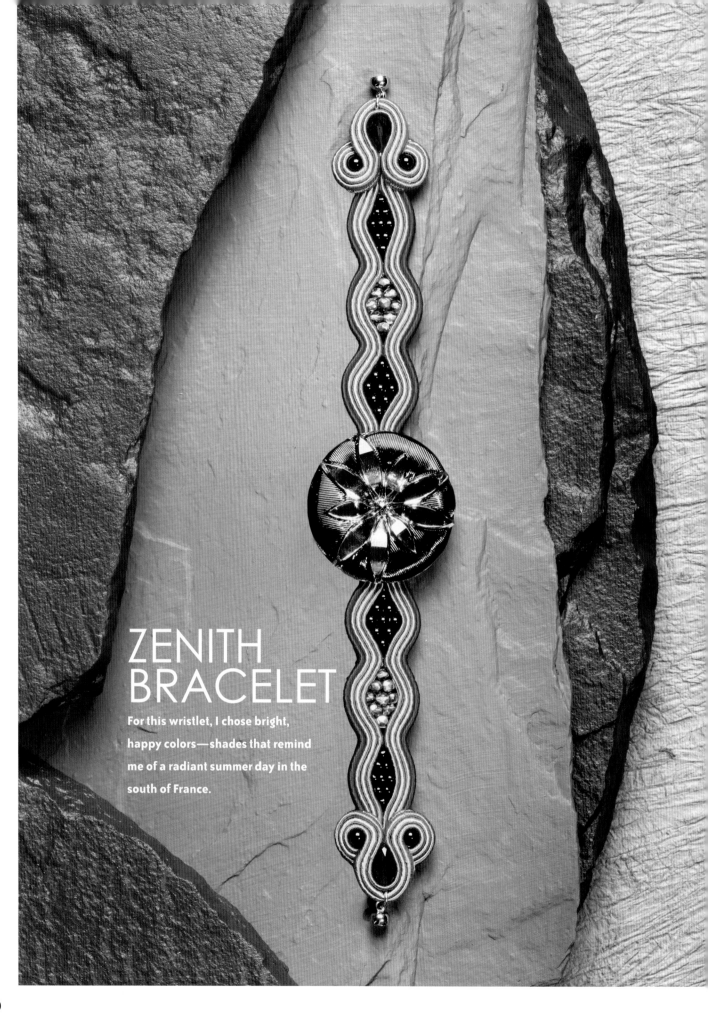

ZENITH
BRACELET

For this wristlet, I chose bright, happy colors—shades that remind me of a radiant summer day in the south of France.

Stitch

Band

1 Cut eight pieces of soutache, two in each color, each 10 inches (25.4 cm) long. With the ends all lined up and the braids facing the same way, sew a short section together with a few stitches, about 1 inch (2.5 cm) from one end. Split the soutache into two even groups, bring your thread out between them, and string on an 8° seed bead (photo a).

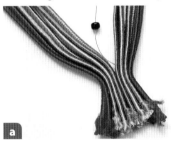

2 Secure the seed bead between the two innermost rows of soutache. Bring the thread out a stitch past the bead and string on two seed beads. Secure the seed beads between the two innermost rows of soutache (photo b).

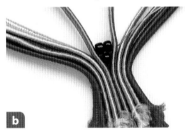

3 To make a diamond-shaped area of beadweaving, continue by adding three seed beads, then two, then one. Finish by sewing the two innermost rows of soutache to each other (photo c).

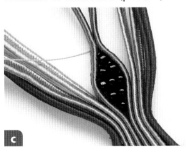

4 Sew the other rows of soutache around the diamond-shaped section of beadweaving, being sure to keep your stitches tiny and in the groove so they won't be visible in the finished piece (photo d).

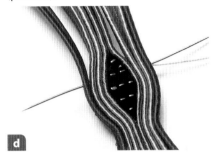

5 Make a number of stitches at the base of the diamond shape to secure all the rows of soutache together (photo e).

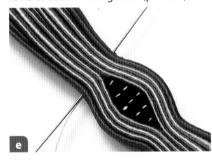

6 Make a second diamond-shaped section of beadweaving beyond the first, but use fire-polished beads instead of seed beads. Photo f shows this step in progress; be sure to stitch the exterior rows of soutache to the innermost ones to complete this step.

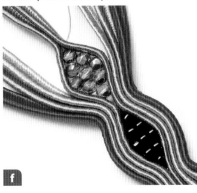

Gather

1⅛ yards (1 m) of soutache in pink, yellow, orange, and red

1 Czech glass button with a shank,* 1⅜ inches (3.5 cm)

18 black glass pearls, 3 mm

18 pale violet Czech fire-polished beads, 3 mm

18 size 8° black seed beads

4 black glass pearls, 4 mm

2 crimson crystal teardrop beads, 9 x 6 mm

1 silver-colored magnetic clasp

2 silver-colored jump rings, 5 mm

2 x 2 inches (5.1 x 5.1 cm) of red leather

Tape measure

Beading thread

Industrial-strength glue

Tracing paper

Scissors

Beading needles

2 pairs of flat-nose pliers

Pencil

*A shank is essential.

Dimensions

¾ x 7¾ inches (1.9 x 19.7 cm), not including focal element

7 Make a third diamond-shaped section of beadweaving beyond the second one, using 3-mm glass pearls this time (photo g).

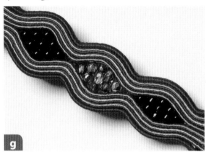

8 Now you'll work on the area to which you'll eventually attach the focal element. Split the soutache into two even groups. Sew each group of braid together for a length equal to the diameter of the button; do not stitch the two groups to one another except at the end of that distance (photo h).

9 Continue making the band, taking steps 2 through 7 in reverse to create three diamond-shaped sections, first using 3-mm glass pearls, then fire-polished beads, and then finishing with seed beads. Sew the button in the designated space created in step 8 (photo i).

Clasp

10 Cut three pieces of soutache—one pink, one yellow, and one orange—each 4¾ inches (12 cm) long. Open a jump ring with two pairs of pliers. Catch one half of the clasp in it, as well as the yellow and orange pieces of soutache. Close the jump ring, then secure all three pieces of soutache together at one point near the jump ring, using just a few stitches (photo j).

11 String on a crystal teardrop, wide end first, wrap the innermost layer of soutache around it, and stitch the trim together at the tip of the bead (photo k).

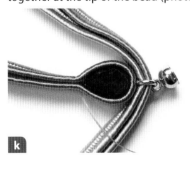

12 Sew the other rows of soutache completely around the bead, using the tiniest stitches possible so they won't show (photo l).

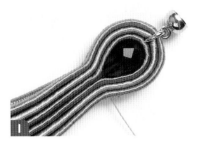

13 String on a 4-mm glass pearl on one side of the teardrop. Surround the glass pearl with the three rows of soutache. Tuck the ends of the soutache to the back of the work (photo m).

14 Attach a 4-mm glass pearl on the other side of the teardrop. Loop all three rows of soutache around it, then tuck the ends of the braid to the back (photo n).

15 Apply glue to all the ends of the soutache, then trim them. Sew down the ends behind the teardrop (photo o).

16 Repeat steps 10 through 15 to make the other half of the clasp mechanism (photo p).

Assemble

17 Place each half of the clasp atop one end of the band as shown and stitch it in place, pricking your needle between the layers of soutache (photo q).

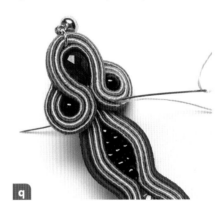

18 Trace and make a pattern for backing each side of the clasp. Cut them out of the leather, and stitch them to the wrong side of the beadwork.

BOLLYWOOD RINGS

With brilliant jewel tones and feminine curves, these rings takes their cues from the riotous color, precious gems, and festivals of India.

Stitch

1 Cut three pieces of soutache, one coral, one gold, and one light beige, each 8 inches (20.3 cm) long. Make a few stitches to secure the three pieces together at their midpoints, making sure that they all face the same direction. String on the glass bead (photo a).

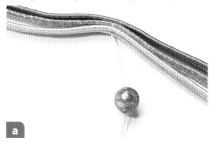

2 String on a seed bead, which will serve as a stopper bead, then pass your needle back through the glass bead (photo b).

3 Making sure your stitches are invisible, sew the three rows of soutache together around the glass bead (photo c). Sew the pieces of soutache together below the glass bead, passing the needle through the seed bead (photo d).

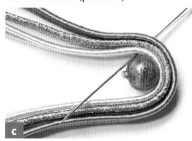

Gather

For the Beige and Coral Ring

20 inches (50.8 cm) each of soutache in coral, light beige, dark beige, and gold

1 coral-colored round lampworked glass bead with gold foil, 6 mm

2 topaz crystal rondelles, 6 mm

2 pale brown crystal rondelles, 4 mm

2 pale brown crystal teardrop beads, 9 x 6 mm

2 pale brown crystal briolette pendants, 7 x 4 mm

1 topaz crystal bicone, 2.5 mm

3 size 15° gold-colored seed beads

1 gold bead cap, 3 mm

1 gold-colored adjustable-size ring with round glue pad

2 x 2 inches (5.1 x 5.1 cm) of beige leather

For Both

Scissors

Tape measure

Beading needles

Pencil

Tracing paper

Beading thread

Industrial-strength glue

Dimensions

1 x 2 inches (2.5 x 5.1 cm)

For the Pink and Blue Ring

20 inches (50.8 cm) of gold soutache

40 inches (101.6 cm) of white soutache

1 chartreuse round lampworked glass bead with gold foil, 6 mm

2 hot-pink crystal rondelles, 6 mm

2 pale blue crystal rondelles, 4 mm

1 rose crystal teardrop bead, 9 x 6 mm

1 cyan blue crystal teardrop bead, 9 x 6 mm

2 pale orange crystal briolette pendants, 7 x 4 mm

1 clear crystal bicone, 2.5 mm

3 size 15° gold-colored seed beads

1 gold bead cap, 3 mm

1 gold-colored adjustable-size ring with round glue pad

2 x 2 inches (5.1 x 5.1 cm) of lilac leather

Note: These instructions explain how to make the beige and coral ring.

4 On one side of the seam, attach a 6-mm rondelle (photo e).

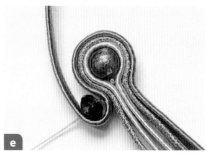

5 Surround the rondelle with the three rows of soutache. Loop the soutache behind the glass bead. Secure the trim by passing the needle between the layers of soutache (photo f).

6 Loop all three pieces of soutache in the opposite direction. In this loop, attach a 4-mm rondelle (photo g).

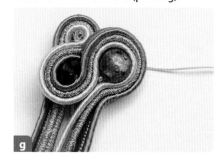

7 Repeat steps 4 through 6 on the other side of the glass bead. Apply glue onto the ends of the braid, then cut off any extra. Set aside.

8 Cut a piece of dark beige soutache 2½ inches (6.4 cm) long. Make a knot and secure the thread ¾ inch (1.9 cm) from one end. String on a large crystal teardrop, narrow end first, then stitch into the soutache as shown in photo h. Pass the needle back through the soutache and the teardrop. Pull the thread tight to surround half the teardrop with trim, and pass through the soutache in such a way as to surround the other half of the bead with trim (photo i).

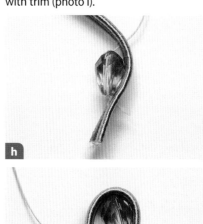

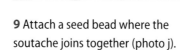

9 Attach a seed bead where the soutache joins together (photo j).

10 Taking care to keep your stitches invisible, attach two more pieces of soutache, first gold, then coral, around the crystal drop (photo k).

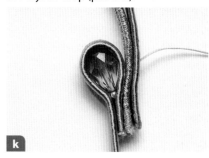

11 Repeat steps 8 through 10 to make a second component, but use dark beige, then gold, and finally light beige braid, as shown in photo l.

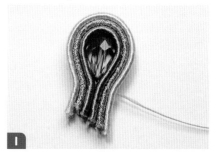

12 Stitch the two smaller components to either end of the larger one, as shown in photos m and n. Pass the needle between the layers of soutache to keep the stitching hidden and to hold all the components securely together on the back of the work (photo o).

13 Attach the briolette pendants on either side of the component made in step 11, as shown in photos p and q.

14 Next, you'll stitch a bicone to the middle of the central element. To do so, bring the needle out under the glass bead, near the seed beaded added in step 2. String on a bead cap and a bicone, then stitch back through the bead cap.

15 Trace and make a pattern for the backing. Cut it out of the leather. The next thing to do is cut a small slit in the middle of the leather, through which you'll push the pad on the ring blank. *Note:* Leather stretches, and the hole should be a tight fit, with gentle pushing required to get the pad through. If the leather slips over the pad easily, the cut is too long.

Slip the pad through from the right side of the leather, as shown in photo r. (The right side should show when the bead embroidery is mounted to the pad in the next step.)

16 Sew the bead embroidery to the backing (photo s).

GYPSY ROMANCE BARRETTE

A sweet breeze blows across this pretty hair clasp. Czech glass, fine chains, and soft color tones come together in a chic Bohemian accessory.

Stitch

1 Use the pliers to fold back the shank on the button (photo a). Sew the button to the piece of beading foundation, apply glue all around the button's edge, and let dry. Leaving ⅛ inch (2 mm) all around the button, trim away the extra foundation. Mark the line of symmetry (photo b).

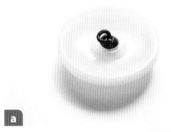

2 Cut two pieces of light gray soutache, each 4¾ inches (12 cm) long. Sew them around the edge of the button, joining them at the line of symmetry and attaching two 3-mm bicones in between the layers of trim (photo c).

3 Cut two pieces of pink soutache and two pieces of violet, each 4¾ inches (12 cm) long, and sew them around the button (photo d).

4 Attach two 6-mm crystals as shown in photo e. Tuck the ends of the trim toward the back. Apply glue to them, wait a few moments, trim them, and attach them to the back of the beadwork.

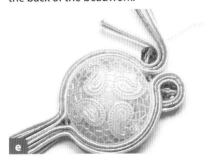

5 Cut two pieces of light gray soutache, each 2 inches (5.1 cm) long, and stitch them to each other. String a white seed bead and a crystal teardrop—narrow end first—onto the thread (photo f).

Gather

1⅛ yards (1 m) of light gray soutache

8 inches (20.3 cm) each of soutache in violet and pink

1 crystal AB Czech glass button with a metal shank, 1³/₁₆ inches (30 mm)

60 to 65 crystal bicones, 3 mm, in a combination of amethyst, lavender, and violet

10 lavender opal crystal bicones, 4 mm

4 amethyst faceted round crystals, 6 mm

2 clear AB faceted teardrop crystals, 9 x 6 mm

1 amethyst crystal pendant drop, 22 x 15 mm

2 lavender briolette pendants, 11 mm

1 amethyst teardrop pendant, 11 mm

2 size 11° white seed beads

Size 11° purple seed beads, 2 g

Size 15° silver-colored seed beads, 1 g

1 barrette finding, 60 mm

19¾ inches (50.2 cm) of silver-colored chain

2 x 4 inches (5.1 x 10.2 cm) of lavender leather

2 x 2 inches (5.1 x 5.1 cm) of beading foundation

Industrial-strength glue

Beading thread

Tracing paper

Chain-nose pliers

Beading needles

Tape measure

Scissors

Pencil

Wire cutters

Dimensions

3¼ x 1¼ inches (8.3 x 3.2 cm)

6 Wrap these beads with the soutache, inserting the needle through both layers of soutache at the bottom of the teardrop. Pass the needle back through the soutache and the teardrop, but not the seed bead (photo g). Pass the needle through one side of the seed bead, then into the loose soutache (photo h). Stitch the loose four layers of soutache together through the seed bead (photo i).

7 Cut a piece of light gray soutache 4 inches (10.2 cm) long and sew it around the teardrop. Begin near the end of the teardrop and add the violet 3-mm bicones as you stitch (photo j). Continue around the bead to the other side of the teardrop (photo k).

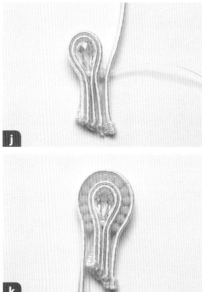

8 Cut another 4-inch (10.2 cm) piece of light gray soutache and add it, keeping your stitches invisible (photo l). Finish the ends of the soutache with glue, and trim. Stitch this entire piece of beadwork to one side of the button, between the round crystals (photo m).

9 Repeat steps 5 to 8 to embellish the other side of the button (photo n).

10 To make a backing, trace a pattern of the entire piece and cut it out of the leather. Make slits in the leather to accommodate the barrette finding, and insert it right side out (photo o).

11 Embellish the edge of the button with a combination of the amethyst and lavender 3-mm bicones (photo p). Stitch the beadwork to the backing (photo q).

12 Embellish the sides of the barrette with 11° seed beads as shown in figure 1. With the needle exiting the groove in the soutache, string on the first bead, then stitch under the last row of soutache on the back of the barrette and up through the groove. Pass your needle under the thread that's exiting the first bead, pull tight, then string on another bead and repeat, working your way completely around the piece.

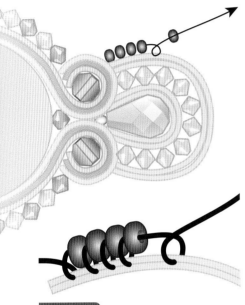

13 Decorate the edge of one side of the barrette with short pieces of chain, beads, and crystal pendants as desired.

DESTINY'S LABYRINTH PENDANT

The spiral is an ancient symbol, rich with meaning. It's dynamic, representing movement, fluidity, and the cycles of life. Every instant of experience enriches us and opens new doors.

Stitch

1 Cut a piece of bronze soutache 15¾ inches (40 cm) long. Knot the thread and make a stitch at the midpoint of the trim. String on an 8-mm bead and a seed bead. Wrap the soutache around the beads and sew the layers of the soutache together using several stitches (photo a).

2 Fold one layer of trim and begin to add a row of seed beads around the beads from step 1 (photos b and c).

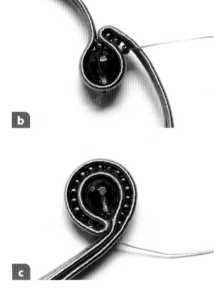

3 Begin wrapping both rows of the soutache around the beads. Be sure to pass your needle exactly into the groove in the soutache. Pull the needle through to the back of the bead embroidery as you work (photo d).

4 Wrap around until the piece measures 1⅜ to 1⅝ inches (3.5 to 4 cm) in diameter. Fold the ends of the soutache to the back, stitch them to secure, add glue, and trim off any extra (photos e and f).

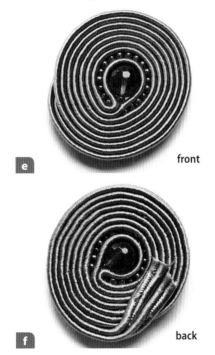

front

back

Gather

3⅜ yards (3 m) of bronze soutache

1⅛ yards (1 m) of beige soutache

19 smoky quartz round beads, 8 mm

11 smoky quartz teardrop beads, 12 mm

4 smoky quartz round beads, 4 mm

34 to 40 smoky quartz round beads, 6 mm

4 brass round beads, 6 mm

4 gold-colored daisy spacers, 4 mm

Size 11° bronze seed beads, 2 g

19¾ inches (50.2 cm) of gold-colored cable wire

4 gold-colored crimp beads

1 bronze-colored S-hook clasp

4 x 4 inches (10.2 x 10.2 cm) of tan leather

Beading thread

Industrial-strength glue

Tracing paper

Tape measure

Scissors

Beading needles

Pencil

Crimping pliers

Dimensions

Chain, 18 inches (45.7 cm) long
Pendant, 2 x 4 inches (5.1 x 10.2 cm)

5 Cut a piece of beige soutache 15¾ inches (40 cm) long. Secure the thread to the midpoint of this piece of trim. String on a teardrop bead and a seed bead, with the wide end of the teardrop against the soutache (photo g).

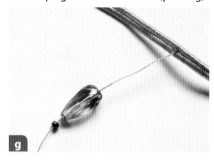

6 Fold the soutache around the teardrop bead and stitch into the soutache to form a point (photo h).

7 Pass the needle back through the beads and stitch together the two layers of the soutache below the teardrop bead. Secure with several stitches (photo i).

8 Cut a piece of bronze soutache 15¾ inches (40 cm) long. Stitch it around the bead as you did the beige piece, *with the midpoint of the trim falling at the point.* Stitch carefully around the pointed end (photos j and k).

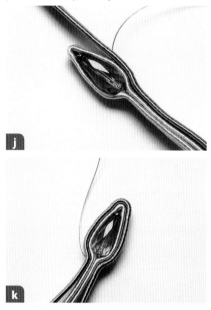

9 Sew the teardrop bead component to the round piece, stitching through all four layers of soutache (photo l), first arranging the teardrop bead component to hide the spot where the ends of the braid are folded to the back of the round piece.

10 Stitch all around the round piece. Apply glue to the ends of the soutache and trim off the excess (photo m).

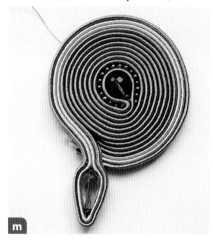

11 At the bottom of the teardrop bead, add a daisy spacer, holding it on with a seed bead (photo n).

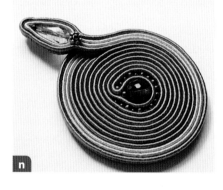

12 Working with bronze and beige soutache, leave 4 inches (10.2 cm) loose as you make another component as described in steps 5 through 8. Add a daisy spacer with a seed bead. Sew together the four layers of the soutache using tiny, invisible stitches. Create a loop and attach a 4-mm bead inside it (photo o).

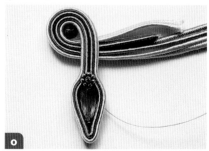

13 Sew the second teardrop bead component onto the round piece as shown in photo p. Apply glue to the ends of the two short pieces of soutache, trim them, and secure them on the back of the component. Continue to work with the long pieces that remain.

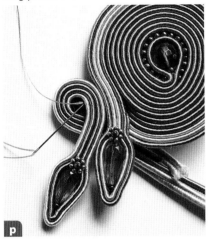

14 Add a row of seed beads using the pieces remaining from step 13 (photo q).

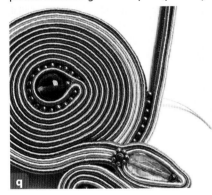

15 Continue this row until it reaches halfway around the round piece. String on a teardrop bead and a seed bead (photo r).

16 Surround the beads with one row of soutache, folding it back to create a sharp point in the trim (photo s).

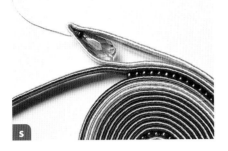

17 Attach the second row of soutache. String on a 4-mm bead (photo t).

18 Loop *just* the beige soutache to the back of the work, apply glue to it, and trim it. Attach a daisy spacer and a seed bead at the bottom of the teardrop bead. Continue working with the remaining end, surrounding the 4-mm bead with it and creating a second, smaller round embellishment (photo u).

19 Attach a daisy spacer and seed bead in the center of the large piece, near the 8-mm bead.

20 Secure the cable wire to the back of the pendant, between the two round components. String on smoky quartz round beads, smoky quartz teardrops, and brass beads until the chain is the desired length.

21 Attach the clasp to the cable wire using crimp beads. Trace and make patterns for the backings of each of the round areas, cut them out of the leather, and sew them to the wrong side of the beadwork.

ATLANTIS
PENDANT

According to legend, a terrible catastrophe
destroyed the island of Atlantis, which
was swallowed into the ocean in the space
of just a day and a night. The story of this
fabled civilization has long fascinated the
popular imagination and inspired
philosophers, writers, poets ... and me!

Stitch

Focal Element

1 Glue the mother-of-pearl pendant to the synthetic suede. After it dries, trim away the suede, leaving a ⅛-inch (2 mm) border of fabric. Cut a piece of mauve soutache 13¾ inches (35 cm) long and use it to create a bezel around the pendant, placing the point of the pendant at the midpoint of the trim. Sew an 8° seed bead between the two ends (photo a).

2 Add two more rows of trim around the first row of soutache, one blue and one gray.

3 Attach a greenish-gray 6-mm glass pearl to one side of the seed bead. Wrap it in three rows of soutache. String on an 11° seed bead (photo b), then sew these rows of soutache to the bezel surrounding the pendant.

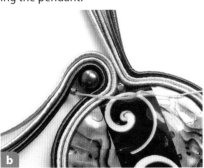

4 Loop the trim behind the pendant and sew a 4-mm glass pearl inside (photo c).

5 Repeat the design created in steps 3 and 4 on the other side of the pendant. Secure, finish, and trim the ends of the soutache (photo d).

Gather

1⅛ yards (1 m) each of soutache in sky blue and mauve

2¼ yards (2 m) of dark gray soutache

1 teardrop-shaped mother-of-pearl pendant, 60 x 45 mm

4 greenish-gray glass pearls, 6 mm

3 blue-gray glass pearls, 6 mm

8 blue-gray glass pearls, 4 mm

Size 8° lavender seed beads, 1 g

Size 11° gray seed beads, 1 g

2½ x 3 inches (6.4 x 7.6 cm) of gray synthetic suede

4 x 5 inches (10.2 x 12.7 cm) of purple leather

Industrial-strength glue

Beading thread

Tracing paper

Scissors

Tape measure

Beading needles

Pencil

Dimensions

Pendant, 2½ x 4 inches (6.4 x 10.2 cm)
Bands, 22½ inches (57.2 cm) long, unclasped

6 Cut a piece of blue soutache 6 inches (15.2 cm) long. Stitch a row of 8° seed beads around either 4-mm glass pearl: leaving the first 1¼ to 1⅝ inches (3.2 to 4 cm) of the trim loose, attach two beads near the pendant, then sew on the rest one by one (photos e and f).

7 Sew on a row of gray soutache (photo g).

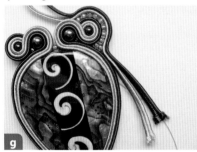

8 Attach a 4-mm glass pearl close to the pendant, and wrap it with two rows of soutache. Tuck the ends of the braid behind the beadwork and secure, finish, and trim (photo h).

9 Sew the loose rows of trim to the soutache that's wrapped around the 6-mm glass pearl (photo i).

10 Loop the ends of the braid to the back of the work. Sew an 11° seed bead inside the loop (photo j).

11 Repeat steps 6 through 10 on the other side of the pendant so the design looks symmetrical (photo k).

12 Attach a seed bead to fill the hole in the pendant (photo l).

13 Cut a piece of mauve soutache 2¾ inches (7 cm) long and attach it around a 6-mm blue-gray glass pearl; add an 11° where the ends of the soutache meet. Sew on a row of 11° seed beads, using mauve soutache. Surround it with a final row of blue soutache (photo m).

14 Sew this element to the top of the pendant element, as shown in photo n.

15 Cut two pieces of gray soutache 4¾ inches (12 cm) long. Making sure to keep your stitching hidden, sew them together lengthwise, curving them as shown in photo o. This element will serve as the bail.

16 As shown in photo p, stitch the bail to the soutache wrapped around the central 6-mm glass pearl.

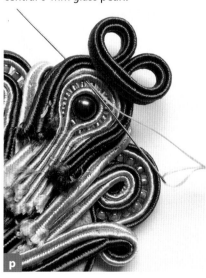

17 Attach an 8° seed bead to fill the gap between the bail and the soutache surrounding the glass pearl (photo q).

18 Cut two pieces of gray soutache, each 19¾ inches (50.2 cm) long. Run them through the bail as shown in photo r.

Soutache Clasp

19 Cut three pieces of soutache, one in each color, each 8 inches (20.3 cm) long. Stitch them together in a curve, being sure to keep your stitching tiny so it won't show.

20 Shape a loop for the closure. Check that the loop fits securely around a 6-mm bead (photo s).

21 To hold all six rows of soutache together securely, stitch through them several times. The loop must be solid and retain its shape (photo t).

22 Just beyond the first loop, make a second, again checking that the bead fits securely inside it.

23 Sew a greenish-gray 6-mm glass pearl between the braid as shown in photo u.

24 Stitch the six pieces of soutache together beyond the glass pearl. Sew a 4-mm glass pearl on one side of the 6-mm glass pearl, and wrap it with three rows of soutache (photo v).

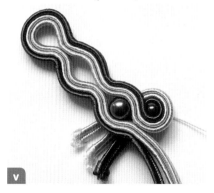

25 Sew a 4-mm glass pearl on the other side of the 6-mm glass pearl. Fold the ends of the soutache to the back of the work, apply glue to them, and trim off any extra. Stitch them down (photo w).

26 You've now finished making half of the clasp. Measure its length, then move on to stitching the other half as follows. Cut three pieces of soutache, one in each color, each 8 inches (20.3 cm) long. Holding them together lengthwise, fold them in half and, starting at the fold, stitch them together through the grooves. This tab should be identical to the length of the finished half (photo x).

x | tab | finished half

27 Sew two blue-gray 6-mm glass pearls to the tab of soutache, placing them so that when they button through the holes, both halves of the clasp lie flat. Finish this half of the clasp as you did the first, steps 23 through 25.

28 Remember the pieces of soutache you cut in step 18? Stitch two of the ends to the back of one half of the clasp, as shown in photo y. Repeat to attach the loose ends to the other half of the clasp.

y

29 Trace and make a pattern for the backing for the pendant, cut it out of the leather, and sew it to the wrong side of the beadwork. Do the same for the clasps (photo z).

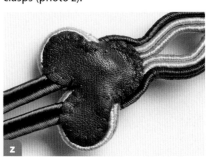

z

CABARET FASCINATOR

A hair comb of red, purple, and fuchsia, festooned with feathers and sparkling crystals,
evokes the fun-loving ambiance of the Folies Bergère and other dance halls of gay Paree.

Gather

1⅛ yards (1 m) each of soutache in fuchsia, dark red, and purple

Crystal teardrop beads, 9 x 6 mm:

    2 pink

    2 red

    1 violet

4 pink crystal rondelles, 6 mm

2 silvery gray crystal rondelles, 4 mm

1 fuchsia crystal bicone, 6 mm

9 size 11° silver-colored seed beads

5 silver-colored filigree flat-top petal bead caps, 7 mm

10 to 15 feathers, such as purple goose biots and fuchsia stripped coque tails

1 silver-colored hair comb, 2⅜ inches (6 cm) wide

1 x 3 inches (2.5 x 7.6 cm) of burgundy leather

1 x 3 inches (2.5 x 7.6 cm) of thin plastic sheet

Industrial-strength glue

Beading thread

Tracing paper

Tape measure

Scissors

Beading needles

Pencil

Dimensions

3 x 2½ inches (7.6 x 6.4 cm), excluding feathers

Stitch

Focal Element

1 Cut three pieces of each color of soutache, each 8 inches (20.3 cm) long. Make a stitch in the midpoint of the fuchsia piece of soutache. String on the violet teardrop, a bead cap, and a seed bead (photo a). Go back through the bead cap, the teardrop, and the soutache, so the seed bead functions as a stop bead (photo b).

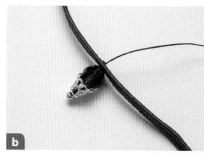

2 Add the two remaining pieces of soutache from step 1 and pass the needle through the teardrop and the bead cap (photo c).

3 Pass the needle through the seed bead as you stitch the six rows of soutache together just beyond the drop (photo d).

4 Stitch together the three rows of soutache that are wrapped around the bead (photo e).

5 On one side of the teardrop, attach a 6-mm rondelle, then surround it with three rows of soutache (photo f).

6 Carefully holding the rondelle in place, sew the three pieces of soutache to the pieces wrapped around the teardrop (photo g).

7 Stitch on a 4-mm rondelle and surround it with the three rows of soutache. Fold all three pieces to the back of the work (photo h).

8 Repeat steps 5 through 7 to attach 6- and 4-mm rondelles on the other side of the teardrop. Fold the ends of the soutache to the back of the work, apply glue to them, trim off any extra, and secure (photo i).

Decorative Elements

9 Cut two pieces of soutache, one fuchsia and one dark red, each 6 inches (15.2 cm) long.

10 Attach the thread 2 inches (5.1 cm) from the end. String on a seed bead, a bead cap, a red teardrop (with the wide end facing the bead cap), and another seed bead (photo j).

11 Fold the soutache around the beads. Create a point in the trim by making a few stitches through the last seed bead strung (photo k).

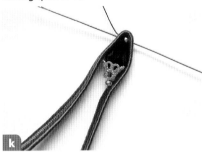

12 Pass the needle back through the drop and the bead cap (photo l). Pass the needle through the seed bead as shown in photo m and poke it through the groove in the soutache.

13 Sew the dark red soutache onto the first row, making sure your stitches aren't visible (photo n). Stitch the four layers together (photo o).

14 Repeat steps 9 through 13 to make a second, identical element.

15 Using pink teardrops and pieces of fuchsia and purple trim, follow steps 9 through 13 to make two more decorative elements (photo p).

Assemble

16 Place the first two decorative elements you made behind the focal element as shown and stitch them securely in place (photos q and r). Apply glue to the ends of the braid, trim them as short as possible, and stitch them to the back of the central element.

17 Cut three pieces of soutache, each 8 inches (20.3 cm) long, one in each color. Placing the braid as shown in photos s and t, sew the three rows around one of the decorative pieces until you reach the bead cap, stitching in the groove of the soutache.

back

sew between the arrows

front

18 Attach a 6-mm rondelle, then surround it with the three rows of soutache you've been working with (photo u). Fold *only* these ends of the soutache to the back of the work, apply glue to them, and trim them (photo v). You will use the remaining free ends in step 19.

19 Using the remaining free ends of trim, repeat steps 17 and 18 to embellish the other side of the focal element (photo w).

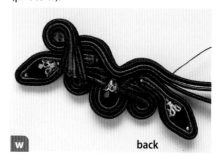

back

20 Sew the third element made in step 15 behind the focal element, curving it slightly. Sew the soutache that surrounds the teardrop to the pieces of soutache surrounding the rondelle (photo x). Repeat to sew the remaining drop to the opposite side of the focal element, making it symmetrical with the piece you just added.

21 Sew the bicone between the pieces added in step 20 (photo y). Pull the thread tight to position the bicone correctly (photo z).

22 Stitch the bead embroidery to the hair comb (photo aa).

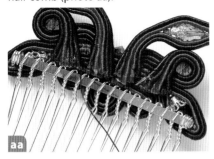

23 Trace a pattern for the backing and cut it out of the leather. As demonstrated in photo bb, it should cover the top of the comb. Use the tracing to cut out a piece of plastic sheet, then trim off ⅛ inch (2 mm) all around. Glue the plastic sheet to the wrong side of the leather. Don't sew the backing on yet.

24 Stitch the feathers to the back of the bead embroidery (photo cc). Trim as necessary.

25 Stitch the backing to the bead embroidery, making sure it covers the top of the comb.

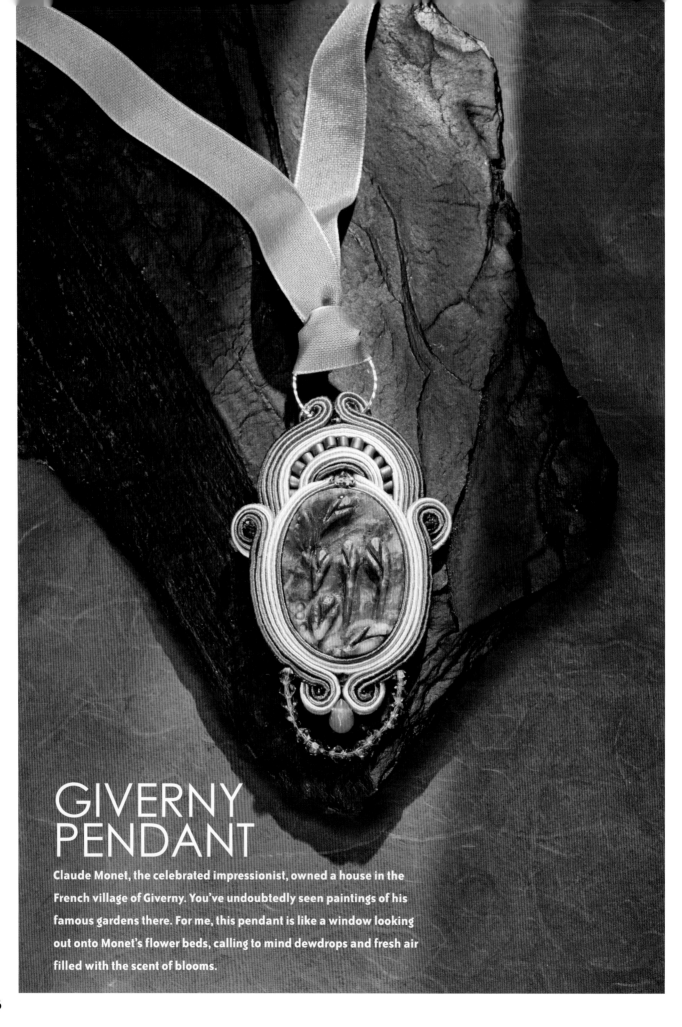

GIVERNY PENDANT

Claude Monet, the celebrated impressionist, owned a house in the French village of Giverny. You've undoubtedly seen paintings of his famous gardens there. For me, this pendant is like a window looking out onto Monet's flower beds, calling to mind dewdrops and fresh air filled with the scent of blooms.

Stitch

1 Glue the cabochon to the synthetic suede and let dry. Cut around the stone, leaving a ⅛-inch (2 mm) border of material all around the stone (photo a).

2 Leaving a 2-inch (5.1 cm) tail, stitch the length of green soutache directly against the cabochon. After attaching it all around the stone, join the trim together with a few stitches. Attach two more rows of soutache around the stone, the first beige and the next light pink. Finish by making a few stitches at the top of the cabochon to secure all the layers of trim (photo b).

3 Cut between six and eight pieces of soutache, each 4 inches (10.2 cm) long, and stitch them into a rounded element incorporating the Delicas, shaping as you work (photo c).

4 Trim the ends of the soutache ⅜ inch (1 cm) away from the cabochon and coat them with a bit of glue so they won't fray (photo d). Place the rounded element at one end of the cabochon, then stitch it to the back of the work (photo e).

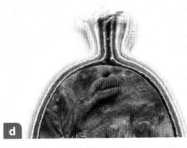

Gather

1⅛ yards (1 m) each of soutache in green, beige, and olive green

8 inches (20.3 cm) of light pink soutache

1 oval carved stone cabochon or pendant, 4 x 3 cm

6 olive-green crystal bicones, 3 mm

8 to 10 blue-green crystal bicones, 4 mm

4 pink crystal rounds, 4 mm

2 pink crystal rounds, 3 mm

1 aventurine briolette pendant, 10 mm

Size 8° matte metallic green iris Delicas, 1 g

2 size 11° dark pink seed beads

3 size 15° olive green seed beads

1 silver-colored metal ring, 20 mm

2 x 2½ inches (5.1 x 6.4 cm) of gray synthetic suede

3 x 4 inches (7.6 x 10.2 cm) of tan leather

Ribbon, 40 inches (1 m) or length as desired

Industrial-strength glue

Beading thread

Tracing paper

Tape measure

Pencil

Scissors

Beading needles

Dimensions

2½ x 3½ inches (6.4 x 8.9 cm), including dangle

5 Stitch lengths of beige, green, and olive green soutache around the cabochon in turn, as follows. Leaving 2-inch (5.1 cm) tails, start beside the rounded element, then work your way along one side of the cab. At the base, just off center, form one curlicue. Take the soutache across the back of the cab, then make a second curlicue, as shown in photo f. Continue attaching the soutache to the other side, working your way to the rounded element.

6 Attach pink seed beads in the curlicues. Between them, attach a 3-mm olive-green bicone, positioned exactly on the line of symmetry of the pendant. As shown in photo g, attach 4-mm crystal rounds close to the rounded element, and then loop the ends of the soutache to the back of the

work. Add a 4-mm bicone with one olive-green 15° seed bead on either side to hide the seam where the layers of soutache meet. If you're using a pendant, embellish the predrilled hole with an olive-green seed bead, stitching it on through the foundation.

7 Cut three 8-inch (20.3 cm) pieces of soutache, two green and one olive green, and stitch them around the rounded element (photo h). At the middle of the piece, make two curlicues as you did for the bottom of the pendant, but instead of adding seed beads, attach the silver ring through the loops (photo i). Attach a 3-mm olive-green bicone between the two loops.

8 Embellish the bottom of the pendant with the aventurine pendant and a dangle of crystal beads (photo j).

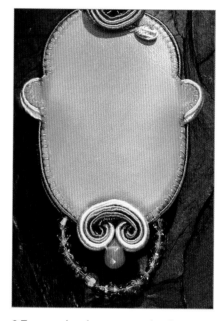

9 Trace and make a pattern for the backing of the pendant, cut it out of the leather, and sew it to the wrong side of the beadwork.

10 To wear the pendant, thread a ribbon through the ring as shown in photo k.

SUNFLOWERS BROOCH

Here's a project you can customize to suit your fancy! I used a large carved stone cabochon, but you can substitute anything with a flat bottom—be it glass, metal, ceramic, or even wood.

Gather

20 inches (50.8 cm) each of soutache in brown, beige, cream, and pale blue

1 rectangular carved jasper cabochon, 45 x 35 mm

Round agate beads:

1 size 4 mm

1 size 6 mm

9 or 10 pearl magatamas, 7 x 4 mm

Size 8° pale blue seed beads, 1 g

Size 11° gray seed beads, 1 g

1 silver-colored pin back, 1¼ inches (3.2 cm)

3 x 3 inches (7.6 x 7.6 cm) of gray synthetic suede

3 x 3 inches (7.6 x 7.6 cm) of blue leather

3 x 3 inches (7.6 x 7.6 cm) of thin plastic sheet

Industrial-strength glue

Beading thread

Tracing paper

Tape measure

Scissors

Beading needles

Pencil

Dimensions

2¼ x 3¼ inches (5.7 x 8.3 cm)

Stitch

1 Glue the cabochon to the synthetic suede. After the glue dries, trim the suede, leaving ⅛ inch (2 mm) all around. Leaving 1¼ inches (3.2 cm) loose at the beginning and starting at one of the corners, sew on a row of brown soutache around the stone, making sure the trim is snug against the stone and that you're passing your needle exactly in the groove (photo a).

2 Finish the soutache bezel by adding three more rows of trim around the first one, one beige, one cream, and one light blue, attaching each in turn. As shown in photo b, don't forget to leave 1¼ inches (3.2 cm) loose at the beginning.

3 Attach the 4-mm bead in one corner (photo c). Surround it with all four layers of soutache, using the other end of the brown piece to act as a fifth layer as shown in photo d. Tuck the remainder of the trim you used to surround the bead behind the work and secure, glue, and trim.

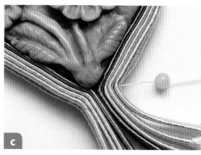

4 Bring over the beige and cream pieces of soutache and sew them around a 6-mm bead without cutting off the excess (photo e). Surround the bead with the two rows of soutache to form a curlicue (photo f). Wrap the ends of the soutache to the back of the work, stitch them down, glue, and trim off any extra.

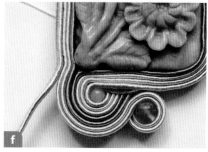

5 Fold the remaining piece of light blue soutache in the opposite direction; you will frame the stone with it. Begin by attaching an 8° seed bead in the fold (photo g). To do so, string it on, pass the needle into the soutache, then pass it back through the soutache and the bead just beside the point the thread originally exited. Pass the needle through all the rows of soutache making up the bezel, and come out on the back of the work. With a stitch or two, sew the piece of light blue trim onto the rows of the bezel just past the seed bead (photo h).

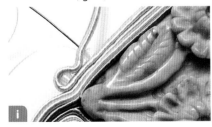

6 Attach a second seed bead beside the first (photo i), then continue adding seed beads as described in step 5 to festoon the side and part of the top of the cabochon. End by folding the soutache to the back of the brooch (photo j). Sew down the end, glue, and trim.

7 Next, embellish around the 6-mm bead using the magatamas. To do this, bring the thread out of the soutache, string on a bead, and pass your needle into the soutache just beyond the bead (photo k). Pull the thread out in front of the bead and pass through the same bead again (photo l). String on another bead and continue the process as you did with the first bead (photo m). Work your way all around the 6-mm bead (photo n).

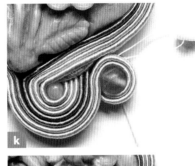

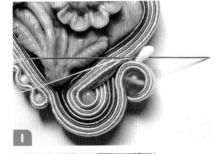

8 Attach a row of 11° seed beads onto the rows of soutache that serve as the bezel where shown in photo o.

9 Trace and make a pattern for the backing and cut it out of the leather. Make slits in it to accommodate the upright shanks of the pin back. Install the pin back through the wrong side of the leather and use a dab of glue to keep it in place.

10 Use the pattern to cut a piece from the plastic sheet, then trim away ⅛ inch (2 mm) all around. Glue this to the wrong side of the leather backing.

11 Stitch the backing to the wrong side of the beadwork.

SECRET PENDANT

At the office or at a party, this pendant is like a true friend. It looks perfectly refined dangling from a fine chain or equally pretty hanging on a ribbon.

Stitch

1 Glue the cabochon to the synthetic suede and let dry. Trim off the extra synthetic suede, leaving ⅛ inch (2 mm) around the stone. Mark the center of the narrow end of the cabochon; this also will be the center of the pendant.

2 Leaving a 3-inch (7.6 cm) tail, attach the length of light gray soutache to the base, directly against the edge of the cabochon. To do so, poke your needle up from the bottom, close to the mark, then catch the groove in the soutache (photo a). Make sure the trim hugs the cabochon tightly and keep your stitches small and close together (photo b). Don't pull the thread too tightly, or you'll damage the soutache.

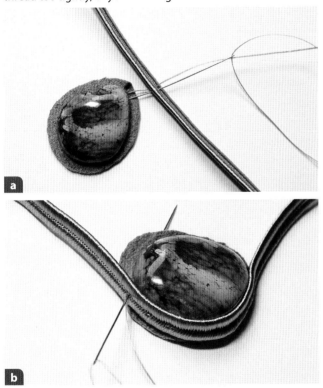

Gather

1⅛ yards (1 m) each of soutache in light gray, metallic silver, and medium gray

8 inches (20.3 cm) each of soutache in aqua and green

1 turquoise oval cabochon, ¾ inch (1.9 cm) long

6-mm freshwater pearls:

  2 light green

  2 dark green

4 malachite beads, 4 mm

1 green opal-finish polygon teardrop pendant, 21 mm

Size 8° gold-lined aqua seed beads, 1 g

4 inches (10.2 cm) of turquoise rhinestone chain, 2 mm wide

2 inches (5.1 cm) of thin serpentine silver-colored chain

Chain or ribbon, approximately 18 inches (45.7cm) long

1½ x 1½ inches (3.8 x 3.8 cm) of gray synthetic suede

3½ x 3½ inches (8.9 x 8.9 cm) of aqua leather

Industrial-strength glue

Beading thread

Polyethylene beading thread (optional)

Tracing paper

Polyester stuffing

Pencil

Tape measure

Scissors

Beading needles

Wire cutters

Dimensions

2⅜ x 3 inches (7.3 x 7.6 cm), including drop

3 Join the soutache together at the center of the cabochon, right above the marked point, tacking the braid together with several stitches (photo c).

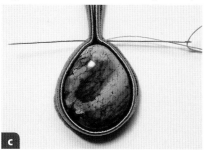

4 Next, attach a row of silver soutache to the light gray trim, then a row of medium gray soutache to the silver braid. Stitch the layers of soutache together where they join (photo d).

5 Sew a light green pearl to one side of the center of the stone, eventually looping all layers of soutache around it (photo e). Make another curlicue with all layers of trim, attaching a malachite bead there. Turn the ends of the braid to the back of the work, finish with glue, trim, and secure.

6 Repeat step 5 on the other side of the cabochon (photo f).

7 Cut a piece of light gray soutache 4 inches (10.2 cm) long and sew it all around the cabochon, catching the rhinestone chain in the seam. To attach, use light gray thread or polyethylene beading thread to keep your stitches invisible. Bring your needle out beside the cabochon and between the rhine-stones close to the outer edge of the chain. Then pass your needle through the groove of the trim you're add-ing (photo g). Pass back through the soutache, pass your needle under the rhinestone chain, and go through the trim encircling the cabochon, pulling the needle out through the foundation.

8 After attaching this row of trim and chain, cut a 4-inch (10.2 cm) piece of sil-ver soutache and add it (photo h).

9 Cut a piece of light gray soutache 10 inches (25.4 cm) long. Sew it around the malachite bead, starting at the midpoint of the piece of trim, stitching down the center of the trim, and insert-ing size 8° seed beads in between. Form a semicircle of six or seven beads (photos i and j).

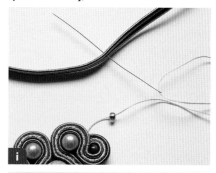

10 Cut 10-inch (26.4 cm) pieces of both silver and dark gray soutache and sew them on as shown (photo k).

11 Using all three pieces of soutache, form a loop on the side of the cabochon and attach a dark green pearl inside (photo l). Hide the short ends of the trim on the back of the work, finish with glue, and cut off any extra.

12 Stitch the remaining long ends of each layer of trim along the back of the pendant and use it to form the loops on the remaining side. Add the seed beads and remaining pearl on the opposite side of the piece as detailed in step 11 (photo m).

13 Add single rows of aqua and green trim around each of the pearls you just attached (photo n).

14 Follow along with photo o. At the bottom of the beadwork, add a row each of light gray and dark gray soutache, attaching them with tiny invisible stitches. At the ends, attach malachite beads. Cut a small piece of dark gray soutache, fold it in half, and stitch it to the top of the work to form a bail. Fold all ends of the soutache over to the back of the work, secure, and finish.

15 Slide the polygon teardrop pendant onto the serpentine chain and stitch the chain to the bottom of the back of the beadwork (photo p).

16 Trace a paper pattern of the pendant and then cut it out of the leather to make a backing. Fill out the back of the pendant with stuffing. Stitch the backing to the pendant. To wear the piece, run a chain or a ribbon through the bail.

SERENADE CUFF

A serenade is a piece of music played or sung under the window of one's beloved. Much like a romantic melody, the soft curves and deep colors in this bracelet were designed to beguile and woo.

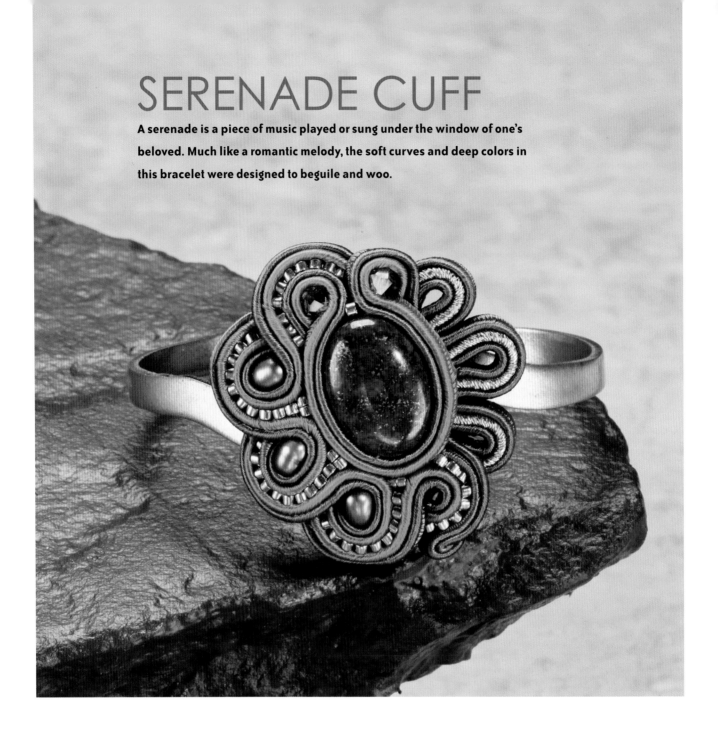

Stitch

1 Glue the cabochon to the synthetic suede. After it dries, trim the synthetic suede, leaving a ⅛-inch (2 mm) margin around the edge of the stone. On the backing, mark the center of the cab.

2 Leaving 2 inches (5.1 cm) free, stitch one row of blue soutache around the cabochon, joining the trim at the marked spot (photo a). Sew on a second row, using the green soutache. Be careful to pass the needle exactly in the groove in the soutache (photo b).

3 Sew on a Delica above the cabochon, between the rows of soutache. Loop back the layers of trim to form a curlicue on each side of the seam. Attach a 4-mm bicone in each loop. Secure the ends of the soutache on the back of the cab, apply glue, and trim any extra braid (photos c and d).

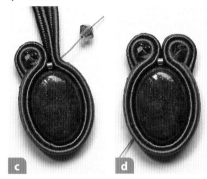

4 Begin stitching a row of Delicas around one of the bicones, using one row of green and one of blue soutache (photo e). When the row of Delicas reaches the cabochon, sew on a freshwater pearl, and loop the layers of soutache around it (photo f), forming a gentle scroll shape. Make a few stitches to secure the soutache on the back of the cabochon. Do not trim off the extra soutache. You'll continue working using these same tails.

5 Make two more scrolls using the Delicas and the pearls (photo g). At the end of each row of Delicas, attach two beads side by side, instead of just one.

6 Make a fourth scroll out of Delicas, ending this one with a blue 3-mm bicone inside the loop instead of a pearl (photo h). Tuck the ends of the soutache to the back of the work, stitch down, apply glue, and cut off the extra.

7 Using blue soutache, add a row of Delicas starting at the edge of the cab (photo i).

Gather

1⅛ yards (1 m) of blue soutache

1⅛ yards (1 m) of green soutache

8 inches (20.3 cm) of gold soutache

1 oval lapis lazuli cabochon, 13 x 18 mm

3 bronze freshwater rice-shaped pearls, 5 mm

2 topaz-colored bicones, 4 mm

1 deep blue bicone, 3 mm

Size 11° gold-colored Delicas, 1 g

Size 15° metallic blue seed beads, 1 g

1 brass cuff with glue pad

2 x 2 inches (5.1 x 5.1 cm) of gray synthetic suede

4 x 4 inches (10.2 x 10.2 cm) of dark blue leather

Industrial-strength glue

Beading thread

Tracing paper

Pencil

Tape measure

Scissors

Beading needles

Dimensions

2 x 2 inches (5.1 x 5.1 cm), focal element only

8 Sew on a second row of blue soutache. At the end of the row, fold the ends to the back of the beadwork without adding a bead. Secure, apply glue to the ends, and trim (photo j).

9 Cut two pieces of blue soutache and one piece of gold soutache, each 6 to 8 inches (15.2 to 20.3 cm) long. Begin sewing them to each other (keep your stitches tiny and invisible), shaping them into a curve as shown in photo k. Continue to stitch, forming three small waves in the strip, each ½ to ⅝ inch (1.3 to 1.6 cm) tall, so your work looks like photo l. Don't be afraid to squeeze the curves to give them the desired shape.

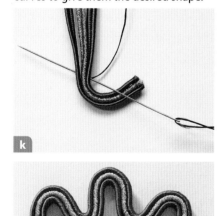

10 Stitch this wavy piece to the back of the cabochon, opposite the curves. Adding the piece fills up the empty spaces on the back of the cab and makes the surface even.

11 Cut two pieces of leather large enough to cover the glue pad on the cuff (photo m).

12 Sew the beadwork to one of the pieces of leather, then glue it to the top of the glue pad. Glue the wrong side of the other piece of leather to the bottom of the glue pad. Stitch the pieces of leather together as you add bead edging (see the box below) with 15° seed beads. Note that the edges will remain unfinished where the sides of the cuff extend from the pad (photo n), so you will add bead edging to the leather in two sections.

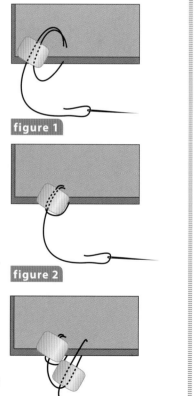

BEAD EDGING

I use this simple bead edging when I need to finish the raw edges of a backing. The instructions and illustrations below are for embellishing a straight edge.

1 Using a comfortable amount of thread on your needle, knot the thread, and pull it through the backing. (Hide the knot between the layers of material if you prefer.) String on a 15° seed bead.

2 Pass the needle up through the backing and then back through the bead only (figure 1), then pull the thread taut (figure 2). Pick up another bead, stitch up through the material, and send the needle back through the bead only, pulling the thread taut after you pass through the bead for the second time (figure 3).

3 Repeating step 2, work your way across the entire edge. Tie off and hide the knot.

figure 1

figure 2

figure 3

Note: When I'm working the stitch around a circular item, I prefer to start by stringing on two beads, and I begin by working the stitch through the *second* bead, not the first. I secure the first bead after I've worked back around to the beginning of the piece.

ARABESQUES NECKLACE

You'll lose yourself in the graceful curves of this necklace, shaped like stylized interlocking branches. This was a frequent motif in Art Nouveau.

Gather

2¼ yards (2 m) each of soutache in burgundy, light blue, blue, and black

1 heart-shaped stone cabochon or pendant, 1½ to 2 inches (3.8 to 5 cm) long

8 freshwater pearls, 6 mm, in a combination of colors to complement the soutache

2 silver-colored two-hole beads with clear AB rhinestones, 10 mm

Silver-colored seed beads:

    size 15°, 1 g

    size 11°, 2 g

    size 8°, 2 g

8 inches (20.3 cm) of clear AB rhinestone chain, 2 mm wide

1 decorative rhodium-plated clasp

2 silver-colored jump rings, 5 mm

3 x 3 inches (7.6 cm) of burgundy leather

3 x 3 inches (7.6 cm) of burgundy synthetic suede

Industrial-strength glue

Beading thread

Beading needles

Wire cutters

Scissors

Tape measure

Wire cutters

2 pairs of flat-nose pliers

Dimensions

20 inches (50.8 cm) long, excluding clasp

Stitch

1 Glue the cabochon to the synthetic suede. Stitch the rhinestone chain to the fabric, surrounding the cabochon (photo a). Cut off any extra chain, then trim away the base right to the edge of the rhinestones (photo b).

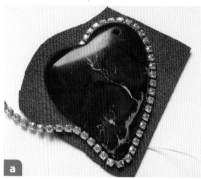

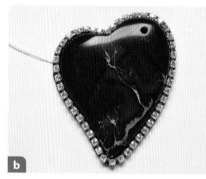

2 Leaving a 2-inch (5.1 cm) tail, attach a piece of burgundy soutache around the entire cabochon, crossing the ends of the trim at the top of the heart and running one end to the back of the work (photo c). Trim the long end, again leaving a 2-inch (5.1 cm) tail. If you're using a pendant, embellish the predrilled hole as desired, stitching on beads through the foundation.

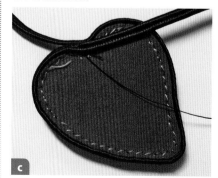

3 Keeping you stitching invisible, attach a second row of burgundy soutache around the cabochon (photo d). Turn the beginning of the braid to the back and trim off any extra material.

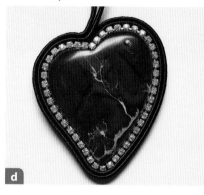

4 Attach a freshwater pearl at the top of the heart by surrounding it with the free ends of soutache. After stitching the layers down, turn the remainder to the back of the work, finish with glue, and trim any extra (photo e).

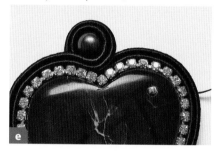

5 Cut four pieces of soutache, each 5½ inches (14 cm), one each in black and blue, and two in light blue. Stitch them around the pearl (photo f).

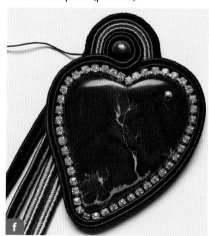

6 Form a loop beside the existing one with a pearl inside it (photo g). Fold the ends of the soutache to the back of the beadwork, finish with glue, and trim away any extra.

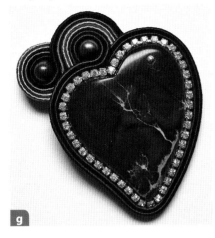

7 Cut four 9-inch (49.5 cm) pieces of soutache, two in burgundy and two in light blue. Tack them together with a few stitches, then sew them together, forming a graceful curve. After 1 inch (2.5 cm) or so, attach a 15° seed bead between the rows of soutache (photo h).

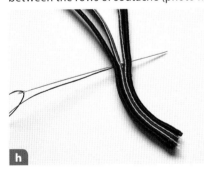

8 Attach additional seed beads: first two or three 15°s, then one or two 11°s, and then a few 8°s. Shape the desired curve (photo i). Gradually diminish the size of

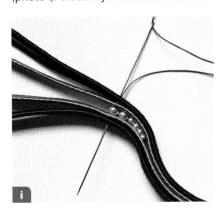

the beads as you sew the four pieces of soutache together (photo j).

9 Wrap and sew all four layers of soutache around a 6-mm pearl, forming a loop as you work. Be very careful to hide your stitching because this part of the necklace will not have a backing (photo k).

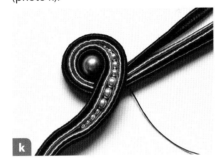

10 Continue sewing the pieces of soutache together, attaching seed beads, freshwater pearls, and a two-hole bead. As you sew, shape the beadwork to form a sort of stem with stylized flower shapes on it (photo l).

11 Make a second stem, altering the design as shown or as desired (photo m). Note that you may need to cut longer pieces of soutache to accommodate a stem with additional decorative elements. To switch colors of soutache, as is done behind the two-hole bead, simply fold a layer of trim behind the bead, finish and secure the

end, and pick up with a new color of soutache. In this stem, the blue trim is replaced with light blue braid.

12 Next, you'll make the two bands. For each band, cut two pieces of soutache, each 15¾ inches (40 cm) long, one blue and one black. Fold each piece of soutache in half and attach the halves of the clasp using a jump ring. Form graceful curves, attaching seed beads of different sizes (photo n). As you work, try on the bands frequently to make sure the asymmetrical design looks balanced.

13 Assemble the elements, making sure to keep the overall shape graceful. If desired, you can wrap one layer of soutache from the bands around one of the elements of the stem, as was done on the topmost blue pearl at the end of the stem at the right.

14 Trace and make a pattern for the backings for the central element and the smaller elements that have cut ends of trim showing, cut them out of the leather, and sew them to the wrong side of the beadwork.

PETRA NECKLACE

Lacework carved into the sides of cliffs—I invite you to travel to Petra, an ancient city cut out of red sandstone in Jordan. A marvel of architecture, this World Heritage Site is a real jewel.

Stitch

1 Glue the pendant (which will be referred to as a cabochon, since that's how you'll use it) to the piece of synthetic suede, then cut it out, leaving a margin of ⅛ inch (2 mm) around the edge of the stone. Use a pencil to mark the center of the top of the stone. This will allow you to keep your beading symmetrical (photo a).

2 Working with the entire length of white soutache, leave a tail 2¾ inches (7 cm) long as you stitch the trim all around the cabochon. Join the trim at the pencil mark made in the previous step (photo b).

3 Add a layer of peach soutache by stitching it to the white soutache attached to the stone, making sure your thread catches exactly in the groove of the trim (photo c).

4 Stitch a piece of gray soutache to the previous row. Stitch all six layers together at the top of the cabochon (photo d).

5 Attach a 6-mm carnelian bead on one side of the join (photo e). Beside it, shape the soutache into a loop, attaching a 4-mm garnet bead inside the loop as you work. Then tuck the ends of the trim behind the work (photo f).

Gather

1⅛ yards (1 m) each of soutache in white, peach, gray, and burgundy

12 inches (30.5 cm) of steel gray soutache

1 rectangular jasper flat-backed pendant, ¾ x 2 inches (1.9 x 5.1 cm)

28 to 32 carnelian round beads, 6 mm

2 carnelian round beads, 4 mm

9 or 10 garnet round beads, 4 mm

6 carnelian oval beads, 14 mm

9 or 10 silver-colored metal tube beads

Size 8° seed beads:

    matte brown, 5 g

    ivory, 2 g

    silver-colored, 2 g

15¾ inches (40 cm) of jewelry cable

2 silver-colored jump rings, 5 mm

1 silver-colored hook clasp

2 silver-colored crimp ends

2 silver-colored crimp beads

2 x 3 inches (5.1 x 7.6 cm) of gray synthetic suede

6 x 6 inches (15.2 x 15.2 cm) of red leather

Industrial-strength glue

Beading thread

Tracing paper

Tape measure

Pencil

Scissors

Beading needles

2 pairs of flat-nose pliers

Crimping pliers

Dimensions

20 inches (50.8 cm) long, excluding drop

6 Arrange the ends of the soutache side by side on the back of the work, to avoid creating a lot of thickness later (photo g). Secure, finish with glue, and trim the ends.

7 Attach 6-mm and 4-mm beads on the other side of the cabochon, as in step 5. Finish the ends as in step 6 (photo h).

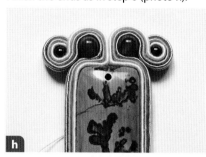

8 Using the length of peach soutache, attach a row of brown seed beads around the 4-mm garnet bead. To do this, start above the garnet bead (photo i) and finish near the cabochon, attaching two seed beads in the same stitch to finish (photo j).

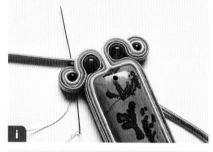

9 Attach two rows of soutache, one in white and one in gray, around the garnet beads, ending with a loop that has a 4-mm carnelian bead sewn into it. Fold the ends of the soutache to the back of the beadwork and secure, finish, and trim them (photo k).

10 Embellish the other side of the beadwork as in steps 8 and 9 (photo l).

11 Using the length of burgundy soutache, embellish the cabochon by stitching on the ivory seed beads (photo m).

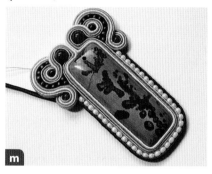

12 Attach three more rows of soutache around the cabochon, one white, one gray, and one steel gray, keeping your stitches tiny and invisible. Tuck the ends of the braid to the back of the work and secure, finish, and trim them (photo n).

13 Leaving a 2-inch (5.1 cm) tail, you'll shape a first wave of seed beads at the top of the beadwork. Begin stitching together three rows of soutache—in burgundy, white, and gray—while attaching another row of brown seed beads, as shown in photo o. Because you're sewing together several layers at once, it's important to keep the stitching especially even.

14 After you've added about six brown seed beads, attach the soutache to a 6-mm bead, as shown in photo p. Without trimming off the ends of the soutache, curl them around the bead you just attached and to the back, then back out, attaching another row of seed beads in between (photo q).

15 Repeat steps 13 and 14 until you've attached three 6-mm carnelian beads. The third and final bead will have only soutache wrapped around it. Create an identical embellishment on the other side of the cabochon. Embellish the predrilled hole as desired, stitching on beads through the foundation (photo r). Set aside this focal element.

16 Attach the crimp end to the jewelry cable, and string on stone beads, metal tube beads, and seed beads as desired.

17 String the jewelry cable through the middle of the soutache surrounding the last bead on the focal element, then secure the cable with a crimp bead (photo s). Do the same on the other side of the pendant.

back

18 Using a jump ring, attach the clasp to one of the crimp ends. Attach a jump ring to the other crimp end. (You'll hook the clasp into it when wearing the necklace.)

19 Trace and make a pattern for the backing of the focal element and cut it out of the leather.

20 Make two bead dangles as desired and sew them to the bottom of the focal element. Stitch the backing to the wrong side of the beadwork.

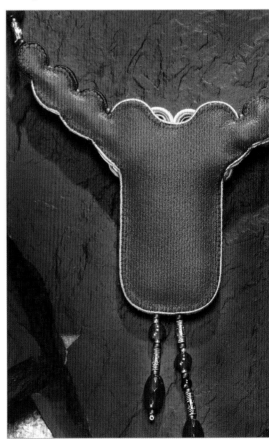

CAPRICCIO NECKLACE AND EARRING SET

A lively, freeform piece of music or a work of art depicting a fantasy scene, a capriccio is sheer whimsy. Embrace spontaneity with these jewels.

Stitch the Necklace

Focal Element

1 Glue the large cabochon to a piece of synthetic suede. After it dries, trim the synthetic suede, leaving a ⅛-inch (2 mm) margin around the edge of the stone. Draw marks to indicate the points of symmetry.

2 Cut two pieces of white soutache each 10 inches (25.4 cm) long. Sew the soutache around the cabochon, joining the pieces at the marks to form the bezel (photo a). Add two additional rows of 10-inch (25.4 cm) soutache, one gold and one white (photo b).

3 As shown in photo c, on each side of one of the joins (and using a three-layer set of soutache), make a loop with a rice pearl inside. Then stitch a curlicue with an olive-green bicone inside it. Tuck the ends of the soutache behind the cab, finish with glue, secure, and trim. Stitch an emerald green bicone right on the join to hide it.

Gather, for the Necklace

4⅜ yards (4 m) of white soutache

1⅛ yards (1 m) of gold soutache

2¼ yards (2 m) of yellowish green soutache

1 oval malachite cabochon, 3 x 4 cm

2 oval malachite cabochons, 1.5 x 2 cm

5 yellowish green freshwater rice-shaped pearls, 7 mm

3-mm bicones:

12 olive green

5 emerald green

2 turquoise blue

4 golden rose-shaped beads, 7 mm

4 green freshwater pearls, 6 mm

1 yellowish green faceted crystal teardrop pendant, 22 mm

26 round malachite beads, 4 mm

Size 8° gold-colored seed beads, 2 g

Size 15° gold-colored seed beads, 1 g

1 gold-colored metal connector

1 gold-colored clasp

2 gold-colored jump rings, 5 mm

3 x 3 inches (7.6 x 7.6 cm) of brown synthetic suede

5 x 5 inches (12.7 x 12.7 cm) of green leather

Industrial-strength glue

Tracing paper

Scissors

Pencil

Tape measure

Beading thread

Beading needles

2 pairs of flat-nose pliers

Dimensions

24 inches (60 cm) long, excluding drop

4 On the opposite side, also attach two rice pearls. Make loops using each set of soutache and attach a 6-mm pearl inside each loop (photo d). Fold the ends of the trim back behind the cab, secure with a few stitches, apply glue to the ends, and trim off the excess.

5 Cut three pieces of white soutache, each 8 inches (20.3 cm). Sew them around the green pearls. Finish each side by attaching a rose-shaped bead (photo e). Turn the ends of the soutache to the back of the work, stitch them down, finish with glue, and cut (photo f).

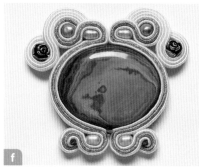

6 Attach an 8° seed bead in the space beside the rose bead. Cut a piece of yellowish green soutache 4 inches (10.2 cm) long. Stitch a row of 8° seed beads to one side of the cabochon (photo g). Sew on a second row of yellowish green soutache. Repeat on the other side of the cabochon (photo h).

Decorative Elements

7 Glue one of the smaller cabochons to the synthetic suede, let dry, then cut all around the stone, leaving a ⅛-inch (2 mm) border. Make a bezel all around the cab using three pieces of soutache, two white and one gold, each about 6 inches (15.2 cm) long. Make loops where the layers of soutache meet, with an olive-green bicone in each loop. Tuck the ends of the soutache behind the cabochon, secure, glue, and cut off the extra (photo i).

8 Stitch a row of 8° seed beads around the olive-green bicone using a piece of white soutache (photo j). Add two more rows of white soutache. End with a green freshwater pearl encircled within the three layers of soutache (photo k). Add a row of gold soutache around the loop. Tuck the ends back behind the cab, stitch them down, apply glue, and cut off the excess. Stitch an emerald bicone to hide the join on this side of the cabochon (photo l).

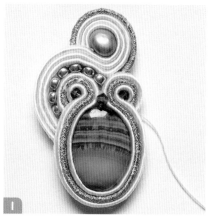

9 On the side opposite the row of seed beads, stitch two 3-inch (7.6 cm) rows of yellowish green soutache all along the side of the stone. Finish by sewing on an 8° seed bead in a loop. Tuck the ends of the soutache behind the stone, secure, glue the ends, and trim (photo m).

10 Repeat steps 7 through 9 to create a second element from the remaining malachite cabochon. Make it a mirror image of the first design.

Assemble

11 Connect the decorative elements to the focal one as shown in photo n, using one bicone of each color surrounded by 15° seed beads. Also embellish the join at the top of the focal element with an 8° seed bead flanked by 15° seed beads on either side.

12 Attach the teardrop pendant to the connector using 15° seed beads and a yellowish green pearl. Sew the connector to the base of the large cab (photo o).

Bands

13 Determine the desired length of each band. Starting with that measurement, here's how to determine how long you'll then need to cut the strips of soutache: Multiply by 2 and add 30 percent.

For example, to make a strap 6 inches (15.2 cm) long, the math works out as follows in inches:
- 6 x 2 = 12
- 30% of 12 = 3.6
- 12 + 3.6 = 15.6 inches

Here's the example in the metric system:
- 15.2 x 2 = 30.4
- 30% of 30.4 = 9.1
- 30.4 + 9.1 = 39.5 cm

14 Using the measurement calculated in step 13, cut three pieces of soutache to the appropriate length, two white and one yellowish green. Attach a jump ring to one half of the clasp. Align the ends of the pieces of soutache, fold them in half, and pass them through the jump ring. Using 12 of the 4-mm malachite beads, make a band with round beads, stitching

the soutache together between each one (photo p shows a start, with five of the 12 beads attached so far).

15 Follow along with photo q. Still working on the band, sew on an olive-green bicone, a rose-shaped metal bead, and a second olive-green bicone. Using one stitch, join the soutache together, add a final malachite bead, and join the soutache together with one stitch. Attach the band to one of the decorative elements as follows: stitch the soutache from the upper side of the band to the soutache that's surrounding the green freshwater pearl. Using the soutache on the lower half of the band, form a loop with an 8° seed bead inside. Tuck the ends of the soutache back behind the beadwork, stitch down, finish with glue, and trim.

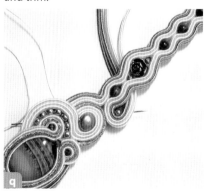

16 Repeat steps 13 to 15 to make a second band and attach it to the other side of the focal element.

17 Trace and make a pattern for backing the focal element and both decorative elements, cut them out of the leather, and sew them to the wrong side of the beadwork.

Stitch the Earrings

Note: Make the earrings mirror images of each other. Stitching them at the same time will make it easier to match the shapes.

1 Cut the synthetic suede in half. Glue one of the cabochons to it, and after it dries, cut off the extra material, leaving a ⅛-inch (2 mm) border of fabric all around the stone. Mark the center top of the cab, which will help you keep the beadwork symmetrical as you stitch.

2 Cut two pieces of white soutache and one piece of gold, each 6 inches (15.2 cm) long. Attach all three rows of soutache around the stone, joining the layers of soutache at the point you marked in the previous step. On either side of this seam, attach an olive-green 3-mm bicone and form a loop, surrounding the beads. Tuck the ends of the trim back behind the cabochon, attach them with a few stitches, apply glue, and trim (photo a).

3 Stitch a row of 8° seed beads around the outermost bicone, using the piece of white soutache (photos b and c). Trim the piece of soutache, leaving a tail of 6 to 7 inches (15.2 to 17.8 cm) to use later.

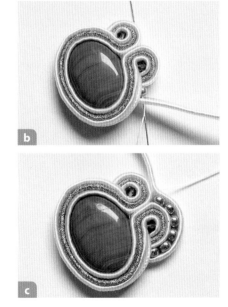

4 Add two more rows of white soutache, leaving a tail of 6 to 7 inches (15.2 to 17.8 cm) from each layer. Finish by attaching a rose-shaped bead, then surround it with two rows of the soutache. String the remaining row of soutache through the ring in the ear wire (photo d).

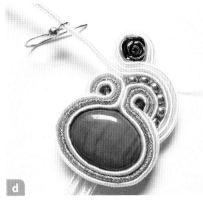
d

5 Sew the loose row of soutache around the rose-shaped bead, being sure to orient the ear wire along the line of symmetry (photo e). Turn the ends of the soutache to the back, sew them down, apply glue, and trim.

e

6 On the side opposite the row of seed beads, add the yellowish green soutache, attaching it to the soutache all along the side of the stone. Attach a second row of the same color. Finish by sewing on an 8° seed bead in a loop.

Tuck the ends of the trim back behind the stone, secure, apply glue to them, and cut off any extra (photo f).

f

7 Stitch on an emerald green 3-mm bicone right on the point where the layers of the soutache meet, above the cabochon. At the base of the beadwork, make a pendant by stringing on a 4-mm bicone, a 15° seed bead, an olive-green bicone, a pearl, and three 15° seed beads. Go back through the pearl, the olive-green bicone, the 15° seed bead, and the 4-mm bicone, and secure the thread (photo g).

g

8 Trace and make a pattern for the backings, cut them out of the leather, and sew them to the wrong side of the beadwork.

Gather, for the Earrings

40 inches (101.6 cm) of white soutache

20 inches (50.8 cm) each of soutache in gold and yellowish green

2 oval malachite cabochons, 1.5 x 2 cm

3-mm bicones:

6 olive green

2 emerald green

2 turquoise blue bicones, 4 mm

2 golden rose-shaped beads, 7 mm

2 yellowish green freshwater rice-shaped pearls, 7 mm

Size 8° gold-colored seed beads, 1 g

8 gold-colored 15° seed beads

2 gold-colored ear wires

3 x 3 inches (7.6 x 7.6 cm) of brown synthetic suede

3 x 3 inches (7.6 x 7.6 cm) of green leather

Industrial-strength glue

Beading thread

Tracing paper

Scissors

Tape measure

Pencil

Beading needles

Dimensions

2 inches (5.1 cm) long, excluding dangle

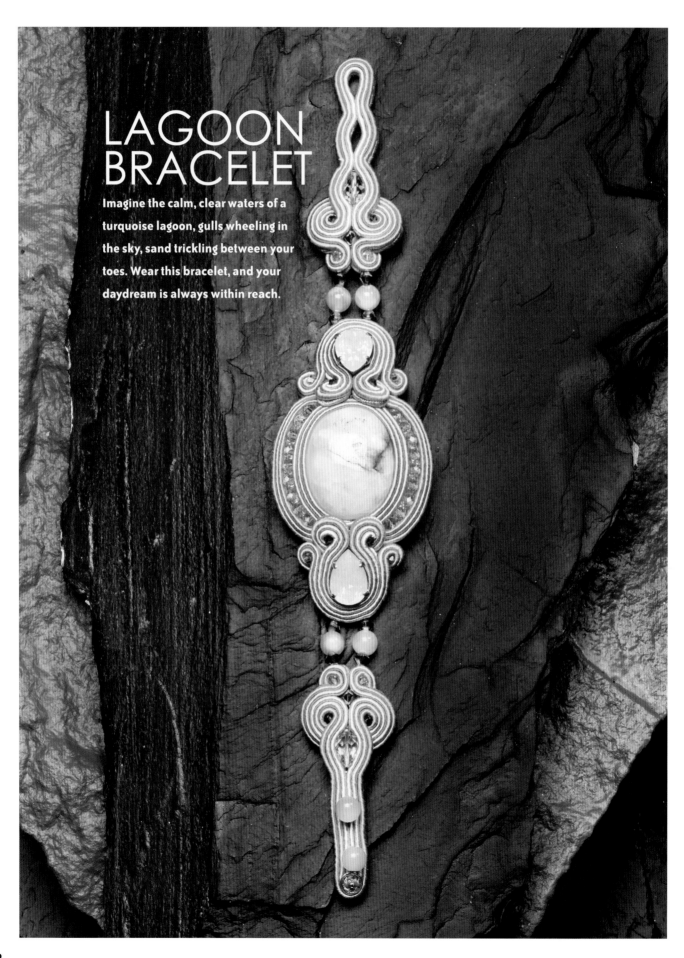

LAGOON BRACELET

Imagine the calm, clear waters of a turquoise lagoon, gulls wheeling in the sky, sand trickling between your toes. Wear this bracelet, and your daydream is always within reach.

Stitch

Focal Element

1 Glue the oval cabochon to the synthetic suede and let it dry. Afterward, cut out the stone, leaving a ⅛-inch (2 mm) border of fabric. Mark the axes of symmetry (photo a).

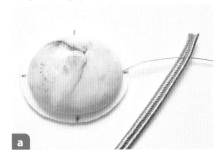

2 Cut a piece of green soutache 13¾ inches (35 cm) long and use it to form a bezel, wrapping and stitching it three times around the cab. Fold the ends to the back of the work, apply glue to them, trim, and stitch in place (photo b).

3 Cut 4¾ inches (12 cm) of soutache in each color, and, passing the needle through the holes in the setting, stitch them to the setting to make a bezel around the pear-shaped crystal. Stitch a green bicone on each side of the tip of the crystal. Surround each bicone with the three rows of soutache. Tuck the ends back behind the crystal, glue, trim, and secure (photo c).

4 Repeat step 3 with the second pear-shaped crystal.

5 Sew the crystal elements onto the soutache that surrounds the oval cabochon. As you pass the needle between the layers of braid, as shown in photo d, be sure not to damage the outer threads of the soutache. Pay special attention to the symmetry. This placement of the crystal elements gives the work a curved shape so it will hug the wrist.

Gather

2¼ yards (2 m) each of soutache in turquoise and green

1⅛ yards (1 m) of sky blue soutache

1 oval chrysoprase cabochon, 30 x 25 mm

2 milky green pear-shaped crystals in silver prong settings, 14 x 10 mm

Crystal bicones, 3 mm:

   8 dark green

   8 light green

18 to 20 pale blue crystal faceted rondelles, 4 mm

6 green onyx round beads, 6 mm

2 pale blue faceted crystal teardrop beads, 9 x 6 mm

10 blue AB crystal bicones, 4 mm

2 x 2 inches (5.1 x 5.1 cm) of white synthetic suede

3 x 4 inches (7.6 x 10.2 cm) of turquoise leather

1 silver snap, ¼ inch (6 mm)

Industrial-strength glue

Tape measure

Beading thread

Tracing paper

Scissors

Pencil

Beading needles

Dimensions

**9 inches (23.5 cm) long
Focal element, 2 x 3½ inches
(5.1 x 8.9 cm)**

6 Stitch a row of rondelles to one side of the oval cabochon, using a row of turquoise trim (photo e). Cut two more pieces of soutache, one green and one turquoise, each 6 inches (15.2 cm) long, and sew them on. Repeat on the other side of the cab (photo f).

7 Cut two pieces of soutache, one green and one turquoise, each 4¾ inches (12 cm) long. Stitch them around one of the crystal elements (photo g). Repeat to attach two rows of trim to the other crystal element.

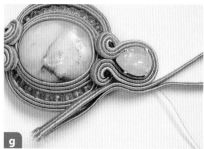

8 On each side of the crystal elements, fold the ends of the soutache to the back, forming them into loops while attaching a light green 3-mm bicone in each loop (photo h).

Soutache Clasp

9 Cut three pieces of soutache, one in each color, each 8 inches (20.3 cm) long. Make a loop as shown in photo i and check that it fits securely around a 6-mm bead. Sew the rows of braid together to form the closure, making sure you keep the stitching hidden.

10 Sew the three pieces of soutache together to form a second loop, once again checking that a 6-mm bead will fit snugly inside (photo j).

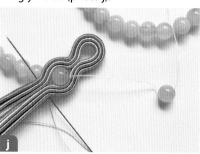

11 Stitch a teardrop bead between the rows of braid. Sew the six layers of soutache together just beyond the bead (photo k).

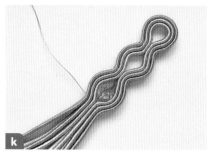

12 Sew a dark green 3-mm bicone on one side of the teardrop (photo l), then wrap the three rows of soutache around it.

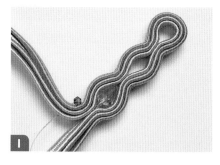

13 Sew a dark green 3-mm bicone on the other side of the teardrop and stitch the three rows of soutache around it. Tuck the ends of the braid to the back, apply glue to all ends, and cut off any excess. Sew the ends to the back of the work (photo m).

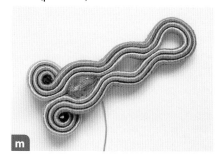

14 Cut two pieces of soutache, one turquoise and one green, each 4 inches (10.2 cm) long. Stitch these around the bicones as shown in photos n and o. Arrange the soutache so all four ends meet below the teardrop.

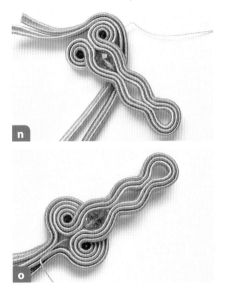

15 Attach a 4-mm bicone where the sky blue pieces of soutache meet. Stitch the four rows of soutache together beyond this bicone. Separate them once again into two sets of two pieces of soutache and form outward-facing loops, each with a 3-mm light green bicone inside (photos p and q). Tuck the soutache behind the beadwork, apply glue to the ends, and cut. Stitch the ends to the back of the beadwork.

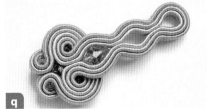

16 To make the other half of the clasp, cut three pieces of soutache, one in each color and each 8 inches (20.3 cm) long. Fold them in half and sew them together lengthwise for a distance equal to the length of the two loops on the finished half. Stitch two 6-mm beads to this tab, lining them up with the loops in the finished half. Finish the tab as described in steps 11 (photo r shows the teardrop bead strung on) through 15. Referring to the photo at the right and on page 22, sew on the snap.

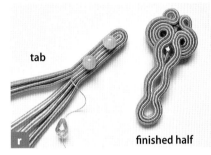

tab

finished half

Assemble

17 Join one part of the clasp to the central part of the bracelet with two strands of beads. As shown in photo s, each strand consists of one 4-mm bicone, one round 6-mm bead, and one 4-mm bicone.

18 Repeat step 17 on the other side of the bracelet.

19 Make patterns to back the focal element and both halves of the clasp. Cut them out of leather and stitch them to the back of the beadwork. Referring to the photo below and on page 82, sew the snap onto the halves of the clasp.

FORCES OF ATTRACTION BROOCH

Opposites attract. The clarity of crystal, the heft of stone, the ruggedness of lava, and the soft weightlessness of feathers—these qualities all come together in harmony with this pin.

Stitch

Note: It's a good idea to use light gray or polyethylene thread to sew on the transparent bicones and use black thread to stitch the black soutache.

1 Glue the cabochon to the synthetic suede. After the glue dries, cut away the suede, leaving a ⅛-inch (2 mm) border all around the stone. Cut six pieces of soutache—two black, two aqua, two white—all 8 inches (20.3 cm) long.

2 Make a bezel by attaching three rows of soutache around each side of the cabochon, as shown in photo a. Where they join above and below the cab, stitch the rows together.

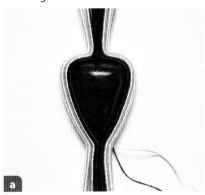

3 Sew the navette above the cabochon, between the rows of soutache, passing the needle between the holes in the prong setting and exactly into the center of the grooves in the soutache (photo b).

4 Stitch a 6-mm bead on each side of the navette. Curve the ends of the soutache behind the crystal, apply glue to them, cut off any extra, and secure them with a few stitches (photo c).

5 Sew a 6-mm bead on one side of the bottom of the cab, then surround it with three rows of soutache. Loop the ends of the trim back behind the cabochon and secure them with a few stitches (photo d).

Gather

1⅛ yards (1 m) each of soutache in black, aqua, and white

1 black triangle-shaped cabochon*, 3 cm long

1 pale aqua crystal navette in a prong setting, 5 x 17 mm

4 round lava beads, 6 mm

2 round lava beads, 8 mm

22 to 28 pale blue crystal bicones, 3 mm

2 pale blue crystal bicones, 4 mm

6 metal rondelles, 5 mm

2 or 3 black ostrich mini feathers, each 4 inches (10.2 cm) long

1 silver-colored pin back, 25 mm

1 x 2 inches (2.5 x 5.1 cm) of synthetic suede

3 x 4 inches (7.6 x 10.2 cm) of black leather

2 x 3 inches (5.1 x 7.6 cm) of thin plastic sheet

Industrial-strength glue

Beading thread, light gray and black

Polyethylene beading thread (optional)

Tracing paper

Polyester stuffing

Tape measure

Pencil

Scissors

Beading needles

* I suggest agate, onyx, or shungite.

Dimensions

3 x 3½ inches (7.6 x 8.9 cm), excluding feathers

6 Sew another 6-mm bead on the other side of the cab, but a little lower than the previous bead you attached to give the piece some visual movement and emphasize its asymmetry (photo e). Tuck the soutache behind the cabochon and stitch to secure. Apply glue to the ends and cut off any extra (photo f).

7 Cut two pieces of soutache, one white and one aqua, both 4 inches (10.2 cm) long. Add these halfway around the soutache surrounding the bead you attached in step 6, making sure to leave tails at both ends. String on a 3-mm bicone (photo g) and loop the two rows of braid around it.

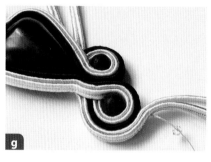

8 On the other end of these two pieces of soutache, string on a 4-mm bicone. Loop all the ends of the soutache to the back of the work, secure them, apply glue to them, and trim off any excess (photo h).

9 Cut two more pieces of soutache, one white and one aqua, each 4 inches (10.2 cm) long. Sew them around the other 6-mm bead, adding a 3-mm bicone (photo i). Turn the ends of the soutache to the back of the beadwork. Secure them, apply glue to the ends, and cut off the excess.

10 As shown in photo j, sew a row of 3-mm bicones along the edge of the cabochon, all the way to the navette, using white soutache.

11 Add two more rows of soutache, one aqua and one black (photo k).

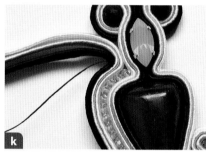

12 Fold the three rows of soutache and sew on three metal rondelles. Sew an 8-mm bead in a loop, close to the 6-mm beads (photo l). Secure the soutache to the back of the work and finish off the ends in the usual manner.

13 On the right side of the cabochon, stitch on another loop made from three rows of soutache, one of each color. String on a 4-mm bicone and surround it with the rows of soutache. Tuck the ends back behind the work, sew them down, apply glue, and trim off any extra (photos m and n).

14 To fill the empty space remaining on the perimeter of the stone, sew on a row of 3-mm bicones using three rows of soutache, one of each color. At the end of the row, fold the layers of trim and sew on three metal rondelles and an 8-mm bead so this side mirrors the one made in step 12 (photo o).

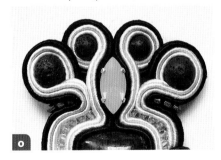

15 Make a paper pattern for the backing (photo p). Cut the pattern in two such that the smaller part covers just the two beads at the top of the cabochon. Cut both pieces of backing out of the leather. Also use the pattern for the large piece of backing to cut a piece of thin plastic, then trim it down by ⅛ inch (2 mm) all around.

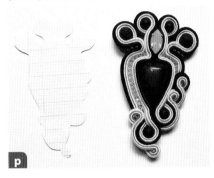

16 Sew the smaller piece of backing to the back of the soutache embroidery. Fill out the empty spaces on the remaining piece with a bit of stuffing (photo q).

17 In the large piece of the backing, mark and cut slits for the upright shanks of the pin back. Insert the pin back through the slits, working from the wrong side of the leather. Secure the pin back to the wrong side using a dab of glue. Glue the plastic to the wrong side of the backing to make it more rigid (photo r).

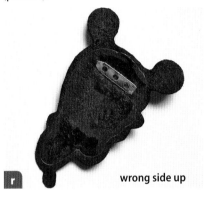

wrong side up

18 Cluster the feathers and sew them to the back of the beadwork (photo s).

19 Making tiny, even stitches, sew on the backing (photo t).

ISHTAR NECKLACE

In Babylonian mythology, Ishtar is the goddess of both love and war. She's at once sensual and strong.

Stitch

Focal Element

1 Glue the cabochon to a piece of synthetic suede. Let dry. Trim off the extra synthetic suede, leaving ⅛ inch (2 mm) around the stone. Mark the axes of symmetry. Using two pieces of soutache, each 8 inches (20.3 cm) long—one peach and one brown—make a bezel around the cab. Stitch the layers of trim together at the join (photo a).

2 Curve two layers of soutache around a 4-mm citrine bead (photo b).

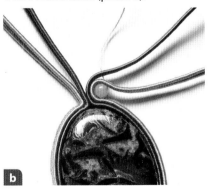

3 Curve the soutache in the opposite direction, catching a 6-mm pyrite bead inside the loop (photo c). Tuck the ends to the back of the work, sew the ends

behind the cab, then trim off any extra soutache (photo d).

4 Repeat steps 2 and 3 on the other side of the cabochon (photo e).

5 Sew two pieces of metallic soutache, one gold and one silver, around a 6-mm bead (photo f). Do the same around the second 6-mm bead.

Gather

3⅜ yards (3 m) of peach soutache

2¼ yards (2 m) of brown soutache

20 inches (50.8 cm) of black soutache

8 inches (20.3 cm) each of soutache in gold and silver

1 oval simbircite cabochon, 3 x 4 cm

2 beige navette crystals in gold-colored prong settings, 15 x 7 mm

1 pale brown flat-back rhinestone, 7 mm

1 citrine leaf-shaped bead, 3 cm long

14 to 16 citrine beads, 4 mm

28 to 30 pyrite beads, 6 mm

16 to 20 gold-colored cube-shaped beads, 5 mm

Bicones:

   2 multihued, 4 mm

   2 metallic bronze, 3 mm

   2 light topaz, 2.5 mm

Size 8° clear, gold-lined seed beads, 1 g

4 inches (10.2 cm) of off-white rhinestone chain, 2 mm wide

1 gold-colored S-hook clasp

4 x 4 inches (10.2 x 10.2 cm) of brown synthetic suede

4 x 4 inches (10.2 x 10.2 cm) of thin plastic sheet

4 x 4 inches (10.2 x 10.2 cm) of brown leather

Industrial-strength glue

Beading thread

Tracing paper

Beading needles

Tape measure

Scissors

Pencil

Wire cutters

Dimensions

Focal element, 4 x 3¾ inches (10.2 x 9.5 cm)

6 Cut a piece of brown soutache 10 inches (25.4 cm) long and add a row of 8° seed beads around the 6-mm bead, starting from the center of the piece of soutache. When you reach the cab, stitch the brown soutache to the rows of soutache around the stone (photos g and h).

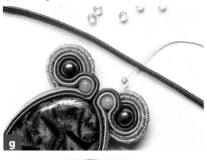

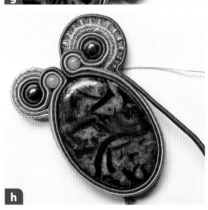

7 Using the other end of the piece of brown soutache, add a row of 8° seed beads on the other side of the cab, surrounding the second 6-mm bead. Add a row of black soutache (photo i).

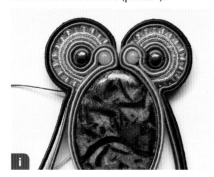

8 To finish off the rows of beads, loop the ends of the soutache to the back, inserting a 4-mm citrine beads in each curved area (photo j). Attach the ends to the back of the cabochon, apply glue, and cut.

9 Arrange the rhinestone chain around the cabochon (photo k) and trim it to the right length.

10 Sew the rhinestone chain around the cabochon, starting from the middle and working outward (photo l). Use two pieces of peach soutache, each 6 inches (15.2 cm) long, one for each half of the cab.

11 Add two more rows of soutache around the rhinestone chain, one peach and one brown (photo m).

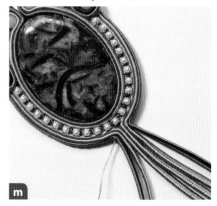

12 On one side of the bottom of the cab, fold back the layers of soutache, catching four 8° seed beads between them (photo n). Curve the pieces of soutache to the back, attaching a 6-mm bead in the loop. Attach the ends of the soutache to the back of the work, glue, and trim them. Repeat to make the beadwork symmetrical (photo o).

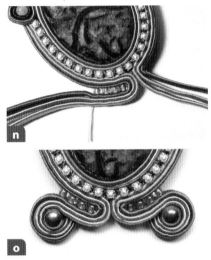

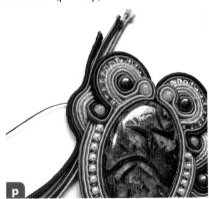

13 On the top of the cabochon, sew two rows of silver soutache around a 4-mm bead. Add another three rows of soutache, one peach, one brown, and one black (photo p).

14 Loop the ends of these last three pieces of soutache to the back, inserting a 6-mm pyrite bead beside the cab as you do so (photo q). Apply glue to the ends of the soutache, cut, and secure.

15 Add a row of 8° seed beads around the loop that doesn't have a bead, using three rows of soutache—two peach and one brown. Then embellish the 4-mm bead on the other side of the cab as you did in steps 13 to 15. Next, glue the flat-back rhinestone to a piece of synthetic suede, let dry, then trim away the fabric, leaving ⅛ inch (2 mm) all around. Make a bezel around it, using three rows of trim—two peach and one brown. Sew this component at the top of the cab, between the two big loops (photos r and s).

16 Sew as many cube-shaped beads as needed to the edge of the cab to fill that space (photo t). Repeat on the opposite side.

Bands

17 Determine the length of the neck band. Cut three pieces of soutache, two peach and one brown, that are twice the desired length plus 30 percent.

18 Fold the pieces of soutache in half, and pass them through the ring attached to the clasp. Make a band that incorporates 4-mm beads, 6-mm beads, cube-shaped beads, and a navette crystal, stitching the layers of soutache together between each bead. Attach the navette crystal fairly near the raw ends of the soutache so it will be close to the pendant (photo u).

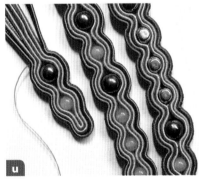

19 Make a second, identical neck band. Sew the bands to the back of the focal component.

20 To make a dangle, string on a 2.5-mm bicone, a 3-mm bicone, a 4-mm bicone, the leaf-shaped bead, a 4-mm bicone, a 3-mm bicone, and a 2.5-bicone. Attach this dangle to the bottom of the beadwork (photo v).

21 Trace and cut a backing out of leather. Use the tracing to also cut a piece of plastic sheet to reinforce the cab. Glue the plastic sheet to the focal element and let dry. Then attach the leather backing to this element.

Wear several pieces of jewelry together for real appeal. Just match your colors so the pairing looks unified. Here I combined Ishtar with a choker.

SUMMERTIME EARRINGS

Light, festive, and stitched up in the colors of the sun and the
sea, these earbobs will make you feel good when you wear
them, as if you are on permanent vacation.

Gather

1⅛ yards (1 m) each of soutache in blue, turquoise, and aqua

2 blue rivolis, 10 mm

4 aqua AB bicones, 4 mm

Size 11° matte metallic blue Delicas, 1 g

Size 15° seed beads:

   metallic blue, 1 g

   silver-colored, 1 g

Size 8° silver-colored seed beads, 1 g

2 silver-colored ear wires

2 x 3 inches (5.1 x 7.6 cm) of dark blue leather

Beading thread

Industrial-strength glue

Tracing paper

Scissors

Beading needles

Tape measure

Pencil

Dimensions

1¼ x 1¼ inches (3.2 x 3.2 cm)

Stitch

Note: Make both earrings at the same time, rather than one after the other. This makes it easier to match them.

1 String 26 Delicas and pass the needle through the first bead strung to form a ring. Working in tubular peyote stitch as described on page 24, add another row of Delicas, for a total of three rows. Add two rows of 15° metallic blue seed beads, then pull the thread tight. Insert a rivoli, right side up, into the bezel, then stitch two rows of 15° seed beads on top to hold the rivoli in place, one row of blue and one row of silver. Tie off the thread (photo a).

2 Leaving a tail at least 2 inches (5.1 cm) long, stitch the length of blue soutache all around the bezeled rivoli, passing your needle through the central row of Delicas (photo b). It's important to catch your needle exactly in the groove of the trim. You want to catch the braid securely against the beads without pulling the thread so tightly that you distort the soutache.

3 Secure the soutache around the bezeled rivoli by stitching it together, inserting a 15° silver seed bead as you stitch (photo c).

4 Leaving a tail at least 2 inches (5.1 cm) long, stitch a piece of aqua soutache all around the blue soutache. Carefully secure the two pieces of trim at the join, using small stitches (photo d).

5 On each side of the rivoli, attach a bicone, then surround each bicone with two rows of soutache (photo e). Tuck the ends of the trim to the back. Apply glue to them, wait a few moments, trim them, and attach them to the back of the beadwork (photo f).

6 Stitch a new piece of aqua soutache all around the rivoli, inserting the 8° seed beads one by one (photos g and h). Don't leave any space between the beads, but don't pull the thread too tightly, either. Otherwise, some of the beads might push up while others sink between the rows.

7 Attach two pieces of soutache, one turquoise and one blue, to the layer of aqua trim surrounding the row of beads, making sure to keep your stitching invisible (photo i). Hide the ends of the trim on the back of the beadwork, securing them as in step 5.

8 Stitch an ear wire in place, between the bicones.

9 Trace and make a pattern for the backings, cut them out of the leather, and sew them to the wrong side of the beadwork.

MIRAGE RING

This bit of bling may be small, but it's sure to garner attention!
You'll soon find that the chic ring matches everything, and
before long you won't be able to do without it.

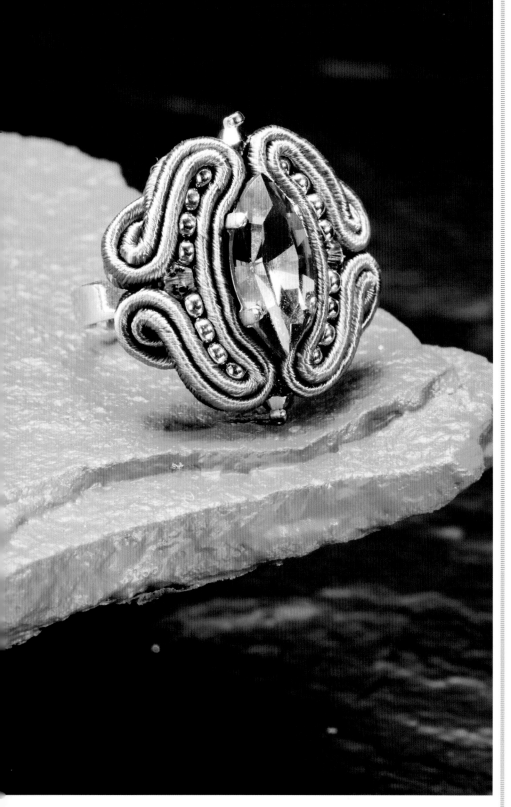

Gather

20 inches (50.8 cm) of gray soutache

1 rainbow green navette rhinestone in a
silver-colored prong setting, 15 x 7 mm

3-mm bicones:

    2 light green

    2 transparent silver-colored

Size 11° palladium-plated seed beads,
1 g

2 size 15° palladium-plated seed beads

1 silver-colored adjustable-size ring
with round pad

2 x 2 inches (5.1 x 5.1 cm) of
black leather

Beading thread

Industrial-strength glue

Tracing paper

Tape measure

Scissors

Beading needles

Pencil

Dimensions

Focal element, 1 x 1 inch (2.5 x 2.5 cm)

Stitch

1 Cut four pieces of soutache, each
4¾ inches (12 cm) long. Sew the
soutache around the rhinestone
setting to form a bezel (photo a).

a

2 Fold back two pieces of soutache toward the center of the rhinestone. Insert a row of four 11° seed beads (photo b shows work in progress).

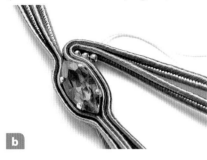

3 Repeat step 2, working from the other end of the rhinestone. As shown in photo c, your thread should exit from between the two rows of seed beads.

4 String on a green bicone and pass the needle through the two left rows of soutache. Then pass the needle through the four rows of soutache to join them (photo d).

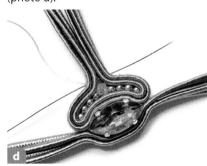

5 Pass the needle through the bicone while passing through the pieces of soutache on the right (photo e). Pass the needle into some soutache near the rhinestone. Fold the ends of the trim to the back of the work, forming a loop on each side (photo f).

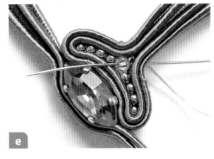

6 Repeat steps 2 through 5 on the other side of the rhinestone (photo g). Apply glue to the ends of the soutache and trim away the excess. Arrange the ends of the soutache on the back of the rhinestone to reduce bulk, and stitch them down (photo h).

7 Sew the transparent silver-colored bicones between the soutache on each end of the rhinestone, holding each on with a 15° seed bead (photo i).

8 Make a pattern for the backing and cut it out of leather. Cut a small slit in the leather to barely allow the ring pad to pass through. Insert the pad through the leather and glue the mounting platform on the ring to the wrong side of the leather. Stitch the backing to the wrong side of the beadwork, capturing the platform of the ring between the layers (photo j).

VERSAILLES BRACELET AND EARRING SET

Put on these jewels fit for a queen, and find yourself transported to the French court, with its white marble staircases, splendid fountains, and glorious gilding.

Stitch the Bracelet

Focal Element

1 Cut two pieces of bronze soutache at least 6 inches (15.2 cm) long. Stitch the trim around the cabochon, as shown in photo a, making sure the pieces of soutache meet along the long sides of the cabochon.

2 Cut two pieces of cream soutache at least 6 inches (15.2 cm) long. Stitch one to each side of the cabochon, attaching them to the previous rows of soutache. Sew a 6-mm glass pearl in each corner, then surround each pearl with cream soutache (photo b).

3 Follow along with photo c. Wrap the bronze soutache around the pearls, then attach 4-mm pearls, using both colors of trim to encircle them. Stitch the ends of the soutache to the back of the work, glue the ends, then cut off any extra trim. On each long side of the cabochon, camouflage the spots where the layers of soutache join by attaching a 3-mm glass pearl flanked with a seed bead on each side.

Bands

4 To determine the length of the bracelet, measure around your wrist; add ⅜ inch (1 cm) for ease, then measure and subtract both the width of the focal element and the length of the clasp. Divide this number in half. Make each side this length, as follows.

5 Cut two pieces of soutache in each color, all 12 inches (30.5 cm) long. Fold each cream piece in half, then use a jump ring to attach one half of the toggle to each (photo d). Fold each bronze piece in half and attach one to each cream piece with a few stitches. Attach a 6-mm glass pearl to each side, between the layers of trim (photo e).

Gather, for the Bracelet

1⅛ yards (1 m) each of soutache in bronze and cream

1 gold flat-backed, faceted octagonal crystal cabochon in a gold-colored prong setting, 14 x 10 mm

16 to 20 white glass pearls, 6 mm

4 white glass pearls, 4 mm

2 white glass pearls, 3 mm

6 size 15° gold-colored seed beads

2 gold-colored jump rings, 5 mm

1 gold-colored toggle clasp

2 gold-colored filigree flat-top petal bead caps, 7 mm

2 x 2 inches (5.1 x 5.1 cm) of beige leather

Beading thread

Industrial-strength glue

Tracing paper

Tape measure

Scissors

Beading needles

2 pairs of chain-nose pliers

Pencil

Dimensions

5½ inches (14 cm) long, excluding clasp

6 Join the strands together just beyond the glass pearl by sewing them with several stitches (photo f).

7 Attach another four (or more, depending on how long you want the bracelet) 6-mm glass pearls to finish each band. Photo g shows a band in process.

Repeat steps 5 to 7 to make a second band.

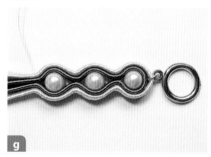

Assemble

8 Stitch the two bands to the back of the focal element.

9 Using new thread, stitch into the empty space at the top of the focal element. String on a bead cap, a 6-mm glass pearl that will tuck into the bead cap, and a seed bead. Go back through the glass pearl and the bead cap, then stitch back into where you started and secure the thread. Repeat at the bottom of the focal element (photo h).

10 Trace and make a pattern for the back of the focal element, cut it out of the leather, and sew it to the wrong side of the beadwork.

Gather, for the Earrrings

1⅛ yards (1 m) each of soutache in bronze and cream

2 gold flat-backed, faceted octagonal crystal cabochons in gold-colored prong settings, 14 x 10 mm

4 white glass pearls, 6 mm

6 white glass pearls, 4 mm

2 white glass pearls, 3 mm

2 pale gold-colored crystal briolette pendants, 11 x 5.5 mm

Size 8° gold-colored seed beads, 1 g

4 size 15° gold-colored seed beads

2 gold-colored ear wires

2 gold-colored filigree flat-top petal bead caps, 7 mm

4 x 4 inches (10.2 x 10.2 cm) of beige leather

Beading thread

Industrial-strength glue

Tracing paper

Tape measure

Scissors

Beading needles

Pencil

Dimensions

1⅞ inches (4.8 cm) long, including dangle

Stitch the Earrings

Note: You may find it easier to match both earrings by stitching them at the same time, rather than completing one and then starting the next.

1 Cut a piece of bronze soutache 8 inches (20.3 cm) long and stitch it to the cabochon, starting on a short edge and running your thread through the openings in the setting, taking care that the soutache presses tightly against the metal. Make a few stitches to join the layers of the soutache (photos a and b).

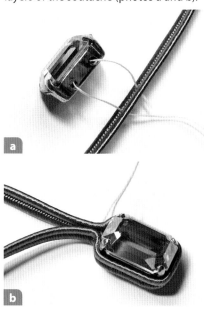

2 Cut a piece of cream soutache 8 inches (20.3 cm) long. Stitch it to the first piece of soutache. Stitch all four layers of the trim together (photo c).

3 Attach a 6-mm glass pearl on one side of the join, and a second pearl on the opposite side. Surround them with the cream soutache in a symmetrical design (photo d). Add the bronze trim, ending each side with a curlicue into which you attach a 4-mm pearl (photo e). Tuck the soutache to the back of the beadwork, glue the ends, and trim them.

4 Use the length of cream soutache and the 8° seed beads to embellish as follows. With your thread exiting on the side of the cabochon, string on a bead, and pass your needle into the groove on the outer layer of soutache (photo f). Pass back through the outer layer of soutache and back through the bead again, taking the needle to the back of the work. Bring the needle back through beside the cabochon, very close to the previous stitch, and add another bead in the same fashion.

5 Continue adding beads as in step 4 until you've worked all the way around. Sew on an additional piece each of bronze and cream soutache, keeping your stitches invisible, then finish and trim off the ends. Sew a 3-mm pearl onto the spot where the layers of soutache join together near the cabochon, adding a 15° seed bead on each side. Stitch an ear wire in place between the 6-mm pearls at the top of the cabochon (photo g).

6 Below the cabochon, attach a dangle as follows: String on a 4-mm glass pearl, a bead cap, and a crystal pendant; pass back through the bead cap and the pearl and into the beadwork (photo h).

7 Trace and make a pattern for the backings, cut them out of the leather, and sew them to the wrong side of the beadwork.

ART DECO EARRINGS

The lines in this design follow the stylings of the Art Deco period, a refined look that incorporated geometry in the service of the decorative arts.

Stitch

Note: You may find it easier to match both earrings by stitching them at the same time, rather than completing one and then starting the next.

1 Cut a piece of beige soutache 6 inches (15.2 cm) long. Sew it around the keystone, going through the holes in the bead (photo a).

a

2 On the narrow end of the keystone, attach a 3.5-mm rhinestone rondelle (photo b).

b

3 Stitch a row of black soutache around the first one, using thread in a matching shade (photo c).

c

4 Attach a black bicone on each side of the rhinestone rondelle, then surround them with the soutache. Looping the braid behind the keystone, bring the four layers of soutache together (photo d). Apply glue and trim the ends, leaving them ⅜ inch (1 cm) long.

d

5 Sew four rows of soutache, two beige, one black, and one silver, in a semicircle above the keystone (photo e).

e

6 Add a row of rhinestone chain to the semicircle, stitching it in between two rows of beige soutache. Then add a row of Delicas, as follows. Referring to figure 1, make a knot and bring the thread out close to the edge of the soutache. String two palladium-plated Delicas, arrange them beside the soutache, and pass your needle

figure 1

through the soutache. Bring the needle out between these two sewn-down beads and pass the thread through the second Delica.

String on two more palladium-plated Delicas, sew into the soutache, bring the needle back out between these two Delicas, and pass your needle through the last bead you attached. When you're partially done, your beading will look like photo f. Go through the row of Delicas again to help them line up nicely (photo g).

7 Cut two pieces of soutache, one beige and one black, each 2⅜ inches (6 cm) long. Refer to photo h for this step. Place the 6-mm rhinestone rondelle at the midpoint of the pieces of braid, stitch in place, then add a bronze bicone on either side. Surround the bicones with both layers of soutache. Fold the ends of the trim to the back of the work, apply glue to them, and cut off any extra (photo h).

8 Add three more rows of soutache around the rondelle—beige, silver, and beige again. Add a row of Delicas all around this component—as you work around, attach the ear wire, centering it above the rondelle.

9 As shown in photos i and j, connect the two components together with one bronze and one black bicone, then sew them to the chandelier drop.

10 Attach a dangle to the bottom of the bead embroidery as follows. Bring your thread out from under the center of the wide end of the keystone, string on a bicone, 10 Delicas, and a crystal pendant. *Note*: The Delicas will pass freely through the hole in the pendant. Pass the needle back through the bicone and into the soutache surrounding the keystone, pull the thread tight, and secure it (photo k).

11 Trace and make a pattern for the backings, cut them out of the leather, and sew them to the wrong side of the beadwork (photo l).

APHRODITE'S GIFT EARRINGS

Born in a wisp of sea foam, Aphrodite is the goddess of love and of beauty. The world's most beautiful women number among her protegées.

Gather

1¾ yards (1.5 m) of light blue soutache

2 deep pink crystal flat briolette pendants, 11 x 10 mm

2 purple rivolis in prong settings, 14 mm

8 off-white glass pearls, 5 mm

4 dark blue crystal rondelles, 6 mm

2 paua shell leaf beads, 45 mm

Size 8° seed beads:

   aqua gold-lined, 1 g

   silver-colored, 4 beads

8 size 15° silver-colored seed beads

2 silver-colored ear studs

4 x 4 inches (10.2 x 10.2 cm) of red leather

2 x 2 inches (5.1 x 5.1 cm) of beading foundation

Beading thread

Industrial-strength glue

Tracing paper

Scissors

Tape measure

Beading needles

Pencil

Heavy needle

Dimensions

1¼ x 4 inches (3.2 x 10.2 cm)

Stitch

Note: You may find it easier to match both earrings by stitching them at the same time, rather than completing one and then starting the next.

1 Trace a briolette twice onto the bead foundation and cut out both shapes (photo a). Set them aside.

2 Cut two pieces of soutache, each 4 inches (10.2 cm) long. Surround a flat briolette with the soutache, making sure it's stitched tightly against the side of the bead (photo b).

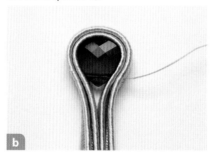

3 Stitch the four rows of the soutache together at the tip of the briolette (photo c).

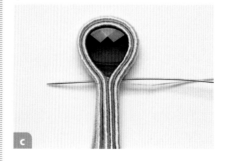

4 Sew a glass pearl on one side of the join, and sew two rows of soutache around it (photo d).

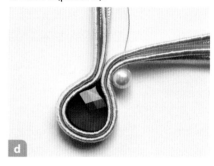

5 Sew another glass pearl on the side opposite the first. Tuck the soutache to the back of the work, apply glue to the ends, and trim (photo e).

6 To prevent the soutache from being seen through the bead, stitch a tracing cut in step 1 to the back of the bead-work, sliding it between the briolette and the trimmed ends of the soutache (photo f). (It's also possible to glue the foundation directly to the briolette).

7 Cut two pieces of soutache, each 8 to 10 inches (20.3 to 25.4 cm) long. Starting at any prong, stitch the soutache around the rivoli, passing the needle through the holes in the setting, making sure the soutache rests tightly against the setting. At the same prong where you began attaching the trim, secure the four layers of the soutache to each other using a few stitches (photo g).

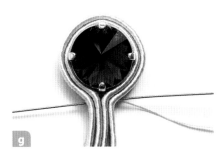

8 Fold two rows of soutache and begin attaching a row of size 8° aqua seed beads halfway around the rivoli (photo h). Repeat on the opposite side of the rivoli; be sure to leave a bit of space where the rows of seed beads meet (photo i).

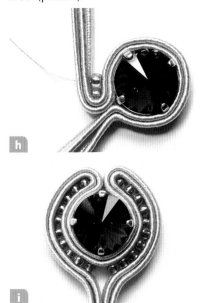

9 Sew two glass pearls on each side of the rivoli. Loop the ends of the soutache to the back of the beadwork, secure them with a few stitches, apply glue to the ends, and trim them (photo j).

10 Attach a rondelle between the two glass pearls, sliding it between the seed beads (photo k). Make a dangle by stringing on a 15° seed bead, a paua leaf, and another 15° seed bead (photo l). Pass the needle into the soutache opposite, so the dangle hangs below the rondelle.

11 To assemble the components, string on a 15° seed bead, a rondelle, and another 15° seed bead. Pass the needle through the beads and the trim several times to hold both components together securely (photo m).

12 To prevent the beadwork from twisting, stitch an 8° aqua seed bead on each side of the rondelle (photo n).

13 Trace and make a pattern for the backings of each of the components and cut them out of leather. Use a heavy needle to pierce a hole in the backing for the top component (photo o). Working from the wrong side of the backing, run the shaft of an ear stud through the hole. Apply a dab of glue to secure.

14 Sew the backings to the wrong side of the beadwork.

CITY OF LIGHT EARRINGS

Imagine yourself in Paris, wearing these earrings. The city teems with nightlife as the glow of streetlights twinkles off the facets of the crystals. All eyes are on you.

Stitch

Note: It's easier to match both earrings by stitching them at the same time.

1 Cut a piece of taupe soutache 8 inches (20.3 cm) long and sew it around the rivoli, passing your needle through the openings in the setting as you stitch (photo a).

2 Use a few stitches to tack the trim together, placing the seam directly above one of the prongs of the setting (photo b).

3 Attach two more rows of soutache, one light blue and one taupe. Keeping your stitches invisible, attach an 11° seed bead in the little space between the rivoli and the trim. Stitch the six layers of soutache together firmly (photo c).

4 Attach a 4-mm glass pearl on one side of the join (photo d). Loop the layers of soutache around the glass pearl and sew them to the soutache surrounding the rivoli, attaching an 11° seed bead below the pearl (photo e). Form a loop out of the three pieces of soutache and tuck the ends to the back of the rivoli (photo f).

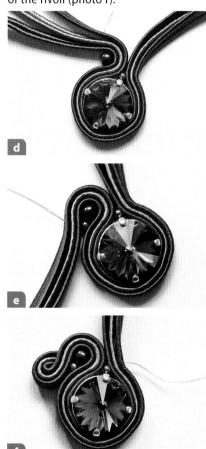

Gather

1¾ yards (1.5 m) of taupe soutache

1⅛ yards (1 m) of light blue soutache

6 inches (15.2 cm) of navy blue soutache

2 sapphire crystal rivolis in a prong setting, 14 mm

4 dark blue glass pearls, 4 mm

8 dark blue glass pearls, 6 mm

8 clear crystal bicones, 3 mm

2 silver-gray pear-shaped sew-on crystal rhinestones, 12 x 7 mm

4 silver-gray faceted rondelles, 6 mm

4 silver-gray faceted rondelles, 4 mm

14 size 11° palladium-plated seed beads

4 size 15° palladium-plated seed beads

2 crystal-topped nail head pronged settings, 4 mm (optional)

2 decorative silver-colored ear posts

4 x 4 inches (10.2 x 10.2 cm) of black synthetic suede

Beading thread

Industrial-strength glue

Tracing paper

Tape measure

Scissors

Beading needles

Pencil

Dimensions

1½ x 3 inches (3.8 x 7.6 cm), excluding post

5 Repeat step 4 to attach a 4-mm glass pearl on the other side of the rivoli (photo g). Finish the ends of the soutache, trim, and stitch them to the back of the work (photo h).

6 Cut two pieces of taupe soutache 4 inches (10.2 cm) long and tack them together at the ends. String an 11° seed bead and a 6-mm glass pearl onto the thread (photo i). Wrap the two layers of soutache around the pearl. Stitch the trim together, passing your needle through the seed bead as you do so. Apply glue to the ends of the soutache and trim them ⅜ inch (1 cm) from the glass pearl (photos j and k).

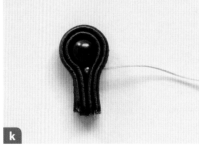

7 Surround another 6-mm glass pearl with two 5-inch (12.7 cm) rows of taupe soutache; attach an 11° seed bead as you work (photo l). Make a loop on one side of the glass pearl, attach a bicone in the middle of it, and turn the ends of the soutache to the back of the work (photo m). Apply glue to them, cut off the extra braid, and stitch in place.

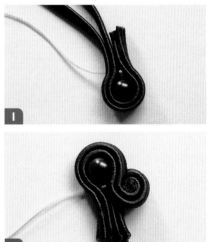

8 Repeat step 7, but make this piece as a mirror image of the first. Set both aside.

9 Glue a sew-on rhinestone to the synthetic suede. Let it dry, then cut it out, leaving a ⅛-inch (2 mm) border of fabric all around. Surround the rhinestone with three short rows of soutache, two taupe and one navy blue, stitching them on one at a time. Make a few stitches to attach all six layers of the trim together where they join at the point of the stone. Attach a 15° seed bead in each hole in the rhinestone (photo n).

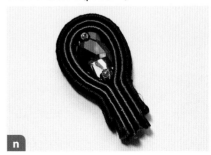

10 As shown in photo o, sew the element you made in step 6 to the element finished in step 5, between the pearls. Then stitch the small elements you made in steps 7, 8, and 9 to the back of the beadwork. Fill each space to the left and to the right of the rivoli by stitching on a 6-mm rondelle (photo p).

11 Cut a piece of taupe and a piece of light blue soutache, each 5 inches (12.7 cm) long, and surround a 6-mm glass pearl with them, attaching an 11° seed bead as shown (photo q). Form a loop on each side of the pearl, attach a 3-mm bicone inside each (photo r), then work glue into the ends of the soutache. Tuck the ends to the back of the beadwork, trim them, and stitch in place.

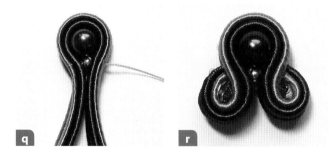

12 Sew the ear post to the piece you made in step 11. Stitch this piece to the rest of the earring, attaching two 4-mm rondelles in between as shown (photo s).

13 Trace and make patterns for the parts of the earring that need a backing and cut them out of suede. Stitch the backing to both parts of the earring, on the wrong side of the beadwork. *Optional:* Before stitching on each of the bottom pieces of backing, you can attach a crystal mounted on a nail head pronged setting to the synthetic suede. (Just push them through from the right side, then fold the prongs over with a screwdriver.) This adds another level of embellishment to the earrings, and in the most unexpected place (photo t)!

MINUET EARRINGS

Romantic, sophisticated, and weightless, these earrings are like the minuet, a graceful dance of the Baroque period and one of the favorites at Louis XIV's court.

Stitch

Note: Stitching both earrings at the same time, rather than one after the other, makes it easier to match them. Don't forget to make them as mirror images of each other.

1 Cut one piece of each color of soutache, each 10 inches (25.4 cm) long, and stitch them around one of the pear-shaped crystals to form a bezel, making sure the pieces of soutache are sewn together at the point (photo a).

2 On one side of the crystal, attach a 6-mm green onyx bead, then surround it with three rows of soutache (photo b). Sew the braid to the bezel and attach a 4-mm glass pearl. Loop the ends of the soutache to the back of the work (photo c). Apply glue, then trim and secure.

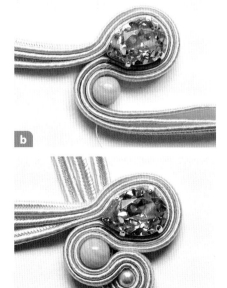

3 On the other side of the crystal, attach a 5-mm glass pearl (photo d). Wrap the bead in the rows of soutache (photo e). Tuck the ends to the back, sew the ends, apply glue to them, then cut off any excess and secure them (photo f).

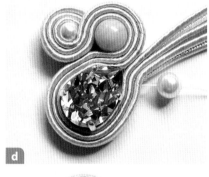

4 Sew a row of 10 bicones around the glass pearl using beige soutache. At the end of the row of bicones, sew the beige soutache to the trim around the pear-shaped crystal (photo g).

Gather

- 1²⁄₃ yards (1.5 m) of beige soutache
- 1¹⁄₈ yards (1 m) of yellow soutache
- 15¾ inches (40 cm) of pink soutache
- 2 green pear-shaped crystals in prong settings, 14 x 10 mm
- 2 green onyx beads, 6 mm
- 8 off-white glass pearls, 4 mm
- 6 off-white glass pearls, 5 mm
- 2 off-white glass pearls, 6 mm
- 20 pale green bicones, 3 mm
- 2 green crystal briolette pendants, 11 mm
- 2 size 11° silver-colored seed beads
- 14 size 15° silver-colored seed beads
- 2 silver-colored ear wires
- 4 x 4 inches (10.2 x 10.2 cm) of off-white leather
- Tape measure
- Beading thread
- Industrial-strength glue
- Tracing paper
- Scissors
- Beading needles
- Pencil

Dimensions

3¼ x 1½ inches (8.3 x 3.8 cm), including drop

5 Add a row of yellow soutache. At the end near the crystal, attach a 5-mm glass pearl. Surround it with the two rows of soutache, fold them back, and sew the rows to the back of the bead-work, then clip the ends (photo h).

6 Cut three pieces of soutache—two beige and one yellow—each 4 inches (10.2 cm) long. Attach them behind the 4-mm glass pearl (photo i) and

stitch them partially around it. Position the work so the pear-shaped crystal is horizontal. Loop the three pieces of soutache to the back of the work and arrange them vertically along the center of the beadwork (photo j). Apply glue to the ends, then trim off any extra braid and secure (photo k). Set aside.

7 Cut three pieces of soutache, two beige and one yellow, each 4¾ inches (12 cm) long. Attach a 6-mm glass pearl to a beige piece, then surround the pearl with the other two rows of trim. As you do, string the outermost piece of trim through the loop in an ear wire (photo l). Stitch the layers of soutache together under the glass pearl, opposite the ear wire. Attach a 15° seed bead to fill in the tiny space between the glass pearl and the seam joining the two middle pieces of trim (photo m).

8 On each side of the 6-mm pearl, sew 4-mm glass pearls. Loop the ends of the soutache to the back, apply glue to them, and cut them. Sew the ends behind the 6-mm glass pearl (photos n and o).

n

o

9 Referring to photo p for placement, assemble both elements together using a 4-mm and a 5-mm glass pearl.

p

10 With the thread coming out of the center of the bottom of the earring, string on one 11°, three 15°s, a briolette, and three more 15°s (photo q). Form a loop by passing your needle through the 11° seed bead, then immediately into the soutache next to it, pulling the thread taut (photo r).

q

r

11 Trace and make a pattern for the backings, cut them out of the leather, and sew them to the wrong side of the beadwork (photo s).

s

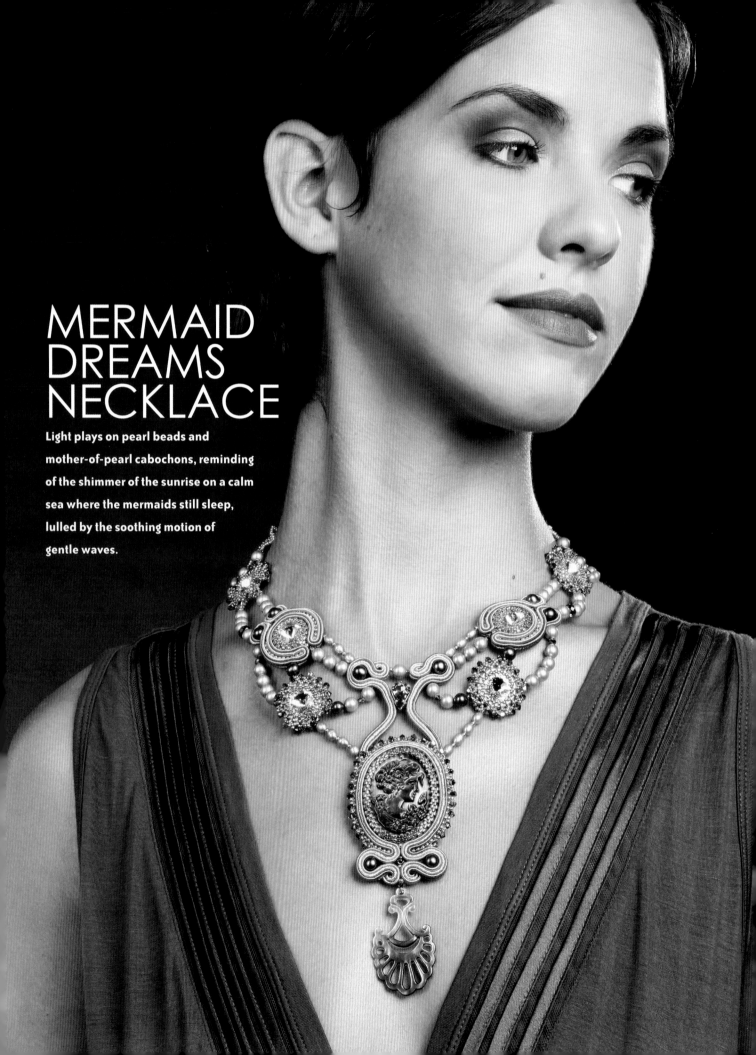

MERMAID
DREAMS
NECKLACE

Light plays on pearl beads and
mother-of-pearl cabochons, reminding
of the shimmer of the sunrise on a calm
sea where the mermaids still sleep,
lulled by the soothing motion of
gentle waves.

Stitch

Focal Element

1 Glue the cameo to the piece of synthetic suede. Let dry. Cut the synthetic suede, leaving ⅛ inch (2 mm) around the cameo. Mark the axes of symmetry.

2 You'll make a bead-woven bezel using two sizes of beads: 11° Delicas and 15° seed beads. Referring to figure 1, make a knot and bring the thread out close to the edge of the cameo. String two palladium-plated Delicas, arrange them beside the cameo, and pass your needle through the synthetic suede. Bring the needle out between these two sewn-down beads and pass the thread through the second Delica.

String on two more palladium-plated Delicas, sew into the synthetic suede, bring the needle back out between these two Delicas, and pass your needle through the last bead you attached. Working in this fashion, completely surround the cameo with a row of palladium-plated beads.

figure 1

Gather

1¼ yards (1.2 m) each of soutache in gray, light gray, and silver

1 mother-of-pearl cameo cabochon, 1⅛ x 1⅝ inches (3 x 4 cm)

1 mother-of-pearl pendant, 1⅝ inches (4 cm) long

1 silver-gray pear-shaped crystal stone in a silver prong setting, 13 x 7.8 mm

10 clear crystal rivolis, 14 mm

12 iridescent black freshwater pearls, 6 mm

45 pale gray glass pearls, 6 mm

30 silver-colored freshwater rice-shaped pearls, 5 mm

3 gray crystal rondelles, 4 mm

2 gray crystal rondelles, 6 mm

140 gray crystal bicones, 3 mm

Size 11° Delicas:

    palladium plated, 4 g

    silver colored, 2 g

Size 11° palladium-plated seed beads, 2 g

Size 15° seed beads:

    palladium plated, 10 g

    silver colored, 2 g

1 silver-colored clasp

10 x 10 inches (25.4 x 25.4 cm) of gray synthetic suede

Industrial strength-glue

Beading thread

Tracing paper

Beading needles

Scissors

Tape measure

Pencil

Dimensions

19 inches (48.3 cm) long, excluding clasp
Focal element plus drop, 4¼ inches (10.8 cm)

3 Next you'll bring the beading up and around the cabochon in peyote stitch, adding a row of silver-colored Delicas. Pass the needle through the first Delica, string on a Delica, and pass the needle through the third Delica. Work around the cameo, stringing on a silver-colored bead and passing the needle in every second bead (figure 2). In so doing, you'll form a ring containing three rounds of Delicas (figure 3). If your cameo is rather thick, add more rounds of Delicas.

figure 2

round 3 →
round 2 →
round 1 →

figure 3

4 Add one or two rounds of peyote stitch using 15° palladium-plated seed beads. This will cause the ring to tighten against the cameo, helping to keep it in position (figure 4). Photo a shows the completed bezel.

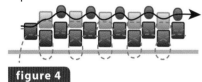

figure 4

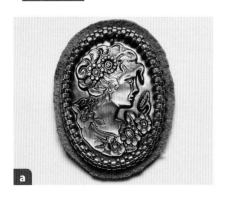

a

5 Cut a piece of light gray soutache 11¾ inches (29.8 cm) long. Sew it completely around the cameo, close to the first row of the bezel, taking care to stitch exactly in the groove of the soutache (photo b). Join the rows of soutache at the base of the cabochon, at the line of symmetry.

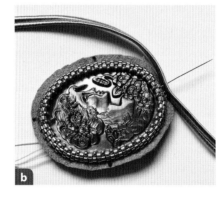

b

6 Attach an 11° palladium-plated seed bead between the ends of the soutache (photo c). Cut two more pieces of soutache each 11¾ inches (29.8 cm) long—one silver and one gray—and stitch them around the cameo (photo d).

c

d

7 Fold back three rows of trim and start a row of beads on the side of the cameo, inserting four 11° palladium-plated seed beads (photo e).

e

8 Sew on a 6-mm black pearl and loop back the ends of the soutache toward the center of the cameo (photo f).

f

9 Repeat steps 7 and 8 on the other side of the cameo. Bring together the layers of soutache below the cameo, loop the ends back to the wrong side, finish with glue, trim, and secure. Attach beads—one 15° palladium-plated seed bead, one 4-mm rondelle, one 15° palladium-plated seed bead—in the space between the loops (photo g).

g

10 Next you'll embellish the edge of the cameo as described below. Add a row of beaded edging using 11° palladium-plated seed beads. Begin with the thread emerging from the last bead in the row created in step 7. String on a bead, sew into the rows of soutache around the cameo, and bring the needle back through this same bead. String on another bead, sew into the soutache on the edge of the cameo, and come out through this bead (figure 5). Work completely around the cabochon.

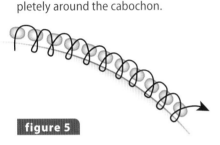

figure 5

11 Add a second round of embellishment using 15° palladium-plated seed beads and bicones. Bring the thread out of an 11° bead added in step 10, then string on a 15° palladium-plated seed bead, a bicone, and a 15° palladium-plated seed bead. Skip a bead and pass your needle into the next 11° bead, passing through the layers of soutache to the back as you do so. Pass the needle back through the same bead. Working in this fashion, embellish around the entire cameo (figure 6).

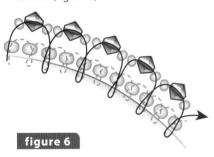

figure 6

12 Below the cameo, attach the mother-of-pearl pendant, using a bicone and size 11° palladium-plated seed beads (photo h).

h

13 Refer to photo i for this step. Cut three pieces of soutache, one in each color, all 10 inches (25.4 cm) long. Sew them together side by side, keeping your stitches invisible and shaping them in a curve. Sew the pieces of soutache to the back of the cameo. Above the cameo, assemble the pieces of soutache as shown in the photo, first adding the pear-shaped crystal. On both sides of the crystal, form curlicues of soutache and attach 6-mm black pearls inside the first loop. Connect the loops with a 6-mm glass pearl flanked by size 11° palladium-plated seed beads. Tuck the trim to the back, glue, trim, and secure.

i

Embellished Rivolis

14 Following the instructions on page 24, and using 36 Delicas in the first round, bead a peyote bezel for each of the 10 rivolis.

15 Embellish two of the bezeled rivolis as follows: add two rows of soutache, one gray and one light gray (photo j). Attach an 11° palladium-plated seed bead where the layers of soutache join.

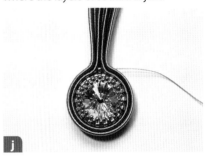

j

16 Fold back an outermost piece of soutache and begin to insert a row of 11° palladium-plated seed beads around the rivoli (photo k). Continue halfway around the rivoli. Then attach the corresponding inner piece of soutache to the first. Repeat on the opposite side. Attach a bicone to fill the gap near the spot where all four ends of the soutache join. Finally, stitch several times to secure the four layers at the join (photo l).

k

l

17 On one side of the join, sew on a black pearl, then loop the ends of the soutache to the back of the rivoli (photo m). Repeat on the other side (photo n). To secure the soutache, make a few stitches on the back of the rivoli, then apply glue and trim (photo o).

m

n

o

18 Embellish six of the bezeled rivolis as follows, referring to figure 7 for steps 18 through 21. String 18 palladium-plated 11° seed beads between the Delicas in the middle row of the bezel.

19 Bringing the thread out of an 11° seed bead, string on three 15° palladium-plated seed beads, and go through the next 11° seed bead. Continue around the rivoli in this fashion.

20 Bring the thread out of a seed bead that's in the middle of a group of three 15°s. String on a 15° palladium-plated bead, a bicone, and another palladium-plated 15°, and go into the seed bead in the middle of the next group of three 15° seed beads. Work your way around the rivoli, adding a total of 18 bicones.

21 Hide the thread by passing several times through the beads in the bezel. Your rivolis will look like photo p.

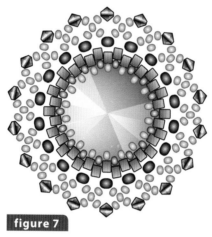

figure 7

p

22 Referring to figure 8 for steps 22 through 24, embellish the remaining two rivolis as follows. String 18 palladium-plated 11° seed beads between the Delicas that make up the middle row of the bezel.

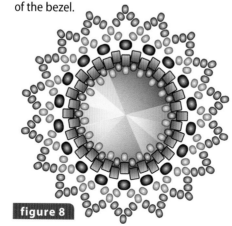

figure 8

23 Bringing the thread out of an 11° seed bead, string on three palladium-plated 15°s, then go through the next 11° seed bead. Continue around the rivoli in this manner.

24 Bring the thread out of the middle seed bead in a group of three 15°s. String on five silver-colored 15°s, then pass your needle through the middle bead in the next group of three 15° seed beads. Keep the thread taut so the seed beads arrange themselves in a point. Bead around the rivoli in this manner.

Assemble

25 Referring to the photos on the next page, assemble all the components of the necklace with glass pearls, freshwater pearls, rondelles, bicones, and palladium-plated 11° seed beads, using seed beads to make loops to attach the clasp. Trace and make a pattern for the backings for five of the components, cut them out of the suede, and sew them to the wrong side of the beadwork.

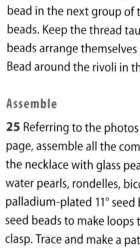

DIVA BRACELET

Light glints off a thousand crystal facets in this exotic cuff worthy of a star.

Stitch

Focal Element

1 Cut a piece of eggshell soutache 4 inches (10.2 cm) long. Knot the thread and secure it to the center of this piece of trim. String on a teardrop bead and a bead cap. Surround the teardrop bead with the soutache and sew the layers together with several stitches (photo a).

2 Add two more rows of soutache, one turquoise and one eggshell (photo b).

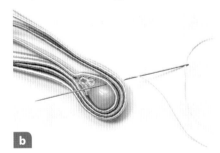

3 On each side of the bead cap, sew on a cube bead and surround it with all three rows of soutache (photo c). Tuck the ends to the back, apply glue, trim, and secure.

4 Sew two more rows of eggshell soutache around the teardrop bead (photo d).

5 Sew 2-mm-wide rhinestone chain atop the two rows of soutache that you attached in the previous step (photo e).

6 Use a new piece of eggshell soutache to sew 3-mm-wide rhinestone chain around the beadwork, as follows. Leave a loose end 1⅝ inches (4.2 cm) long. Pass the needle between the rhinestones, bringing it back under the chain for the next stitch (photo f).

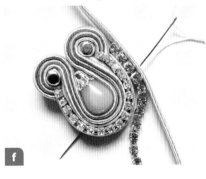

Gather

2¼ yards (2 m) each of soutache in eggshell and turquoise

2 amazonite teardrop beads, 10 mm

4 amazonite rondelles, 8 mm

20 to 24 silver-colored cube beads, 5 mm

2 green bicones, 3 mm

11 size 8° silver-colored seed beads

8 inches (20.3 cm) of clear AB rhinestone chain, 2 mm wide

8 inches (20.3 cm) of light blue rhinestone chain, 3 mm wide

2 silver-colored filigree flat-top petal bead caps, 7 mm

1 silver-colored magnetic clasp

4 silver-colored oval jump rings, 5 mm

4 x 4 inches (10.2 cm) of light blue leather

Beading thread

Tracing paper

Tape measure

Scissors

Beading needles

Industrial-strength glue

Wire cutters

Pencil

2 pairs of flat-nose pliers

Wire cutters

Dimensions

2½ x 6½ inches (6.4 x 16.5 cm)

7 Add two more rows of soutache, one turquoise and one eggshell. Loop the loose ends on each side to the back of the beadwork, with a seed bead in each loop (photo g). Finish and secure the ends of the trim.

8 Cut three pieces of soutache each 2¾ inches (7 cm) long—two eggshell and one turquoise. Sew them around a second teardrop bead and its bead cap. Cut three more rows of soutache, each 4 inches (10.4 cm) long—two turquoise and one eggshell—and use them to add a piece of 3-mm-wide rhinestone chain around the teardrop bead (photo h).

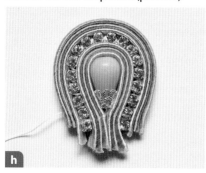

9 Cut two longer rows of soutache each 5½ inches (14 cm) long, one eggshell and one turquoise. Stitch them on (photo i).

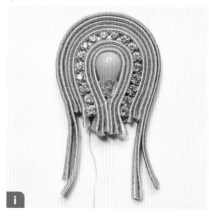

10 Sew 2-mm-wide rhinestone chain atop the two rows of turquoise soutache (photo j).

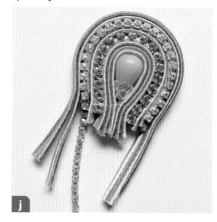

11 Sew together the two pieces of beadwork you've assembled, as follows. Arrange the piece with the cube beads on top. Sew through all the pieces with the needle passing exactly between the rows of soutache. Be careful not to damage the trim (photo k).

12 Loop the loose ends of the lower piece—the one without cube beads—to the back of the beadwork, attaching a seed bead in each loop. With your thread exiting from between the space between the two pieces of beadwork (photo l), attach a 3-mm bicone on each side.

13 Cut three new pieces of soutache each 5 inches (12.7 cm) long—two eggshell and one turquoise. Leave loose ends 2 inches (5.1 cm) long. Sew the soutache onto the lower piece of beadwork, around the loop that surrounds the seed bead (photo m).

14 Where the two pieces of beadwork are joined, make a curlicue and sew a 5-mm cube bead inside it. Pass the ends across the back of the beadwork. Attach a seed bead beside the cube bead, between the two components (photo n).

15 On the opposite side of the beadwork, make a mirror image of the design formed in steps 13 and 14, using the remaining soutache that you passed behind the beadwork. Stitch the ends of the trim to the back of the beadwork, apply glue to them, and cut off the excess. Add a seed bead in the center of this piece of beadwork, between the teardrop beads at the center the connected pieces of beadwork.

Bands

16 Cut three pieces of soutache each 4 inches (10.2 cm) long—two eggshell and one turquoise. Surround a rondelle with them, sewing all the layers of the soutache together at the join as shown (photo o).

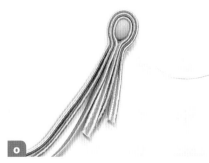

17 Sew two cube beads on each side of the rondelle. Loop the ends of the soutache to the back of the work. Apply glue to them, cut them, and sew them behind the rondelle (photo p).

18 Sew a piece of 3-mm rhinestone chain around the rondelle using eggshell trim (photo q). Finish and secure the ends of the trim.

19 Cut two pieces of turquoise soutache each 2⅜ inches (6.5 cm) long. Apply glue to the ends. Slide them through a jump ring attached to one half of the clasp. Sew both pieces of soutache around the rhinestone chain (photo r).

20 Surround another rondelle with 3-inch (7.6 cm) rows of soutache, two eggshell and one turquoise (photo s). Stitch a piece of 2-mm rhinestone chain around the bead, directly atop the rows of soutache.

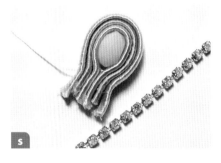

21 Make a band using three cube beads stitched between four rows of soutache (photo t); cut the first two rows of soutache (one in each color) to about 4 inches (10.2 cm). Use long lengths of soutache for the other two rows and leave them long because you'll use them in the next step.

Note: You can adjust the length of the band by adding more cube beads, bearing in mind that with three cube beads in this component the cuff will measure 6½ inches (16.5 cm).

22 Sew this band to the focal element as shown in photo u. Using the two longer pieces of soutache, make a loop, attaching a seed bead inside it.

23 Repeat step 21 to make a second band. Sew it on the same side of the focal element, below the seed-bead loop. Stitch the piece made in step 20 between the bands. Secure these elements together by sewing them onto the back of the beadwork, as shown in photo v.

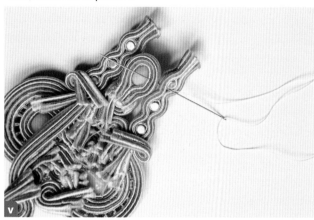

24 Stitch the element with the clasp to the unfinished ends of the two bands (photo w).

25 Repeat steps 16 through 24 to finish the other side of the cuff. Trace and make patterns for the backings for the focal element and the two smaller pieces of beadwork that are part of the clasp components, cut them out of the leather, and sew them to the wrong side of the beadwork.

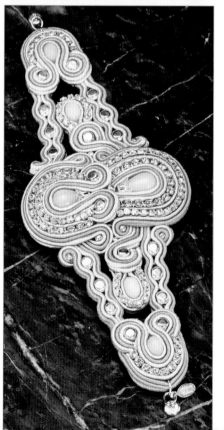

MOON RIVER NECKLACE

This spectacular ornament is the stuff of fairy princesses. The opalescent nuances of the crystals combine with the smooth, velvety look of pearl after pearl for a necklace you'll want to wear on the most special of occasions.

Gather

8 yards (7.2 m) of white soutache

6 yards (5.4 m) of aqua soutache

Opalescent rhinestones:

> **1 oval crystal in a silver prong setting, 18 x 13 mm**

> **1 oval crystal in a silver prong setting, 8 x 6 mm**

> **8 pear-shaped crystals in silver prong settings, 14 x 10 mm**

> **1 faceted polygon pendant, 17 mm**

> **1 faceted polygon pendant, 13 mm**

Glass pearls:

> **42 white, 6 mm**

> **84 white, 4 mm**

> **58 white, 3 mm**

2 green crystal bicones, 4 mm

44 opalescent crystal bicones, 3 mm

28 inches (71.1 cm) of turquoise rhinestone chain, 2 mm wide

Size 8° opalescent silver-lined seed beads, 5 g

Size 11° silver-colored seed beads, 1 g

1 silver-colored filigree bead cap, 7 mm

1 rhodium-plated 3-hole clasp, 24 mm, with an extender chain

1 silver-colored triangle jump ring, 5 mm

3 x 15 inches (7.6 x 38.1 cm) of light blue leather

3 x 15 inches (7.6 x 38.1 cm) of thin plastic sheet (optional)

Tape measure

Beading thread, white and light gray

Industrial-strength glue

Tracing paper

Scissors

Beading needles

Pencil

Wire cutters

Dimensions

18 inches (45.7 cm) long

Stitch

Focal Element

1 Cut a piece of white soutache 8 inches (20.3 cm) long. Create a bezel by sewing it around the 18 x 13-mm oval rhinestone, with the braid joining at one end of the stone as shown. Attach an 11° seed bead to fill the gap near the join, then add two more rows of soutache, one aqua and one white (photo a).

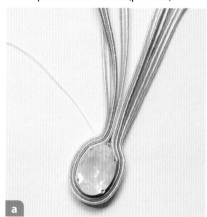

2 Sew a 4-mm glass pearl on one side of the join, and wrap all three rows of soutache around it. Stitch the rows of soutache to the bezel. Attach an 11° seed bead in the gap below the pearl (photo b). Loop the ends of the soutache to the back of the work, sewing a 6-mm glass pearl inside the loop (photo c). Apply glue to the ends of the braid, trim, and secure. Repeat on the other side to make the element symmetrical (photo d).

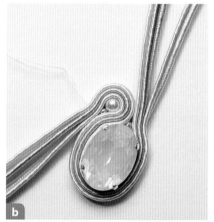

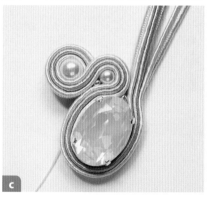

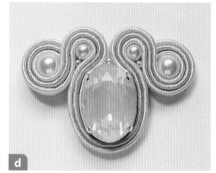

3 Cut a piece of white soutache 4 inches (10.2 cm) long. Use it to sew a row of 8° seed beads around the 6-mm pearl (photo e). Finish the row near the oval rhinestone; attach two seed beads. Add a second row of soutache, using aqua trim. Loop the ends of the soutache to the back, attaching a 4-mm glass pearl inside this loop. Apply glue to the ends of the braid, cut off any extra, and sew them down to the back of the piece. Repeat on the other side (photo f).

4 Cut a piece of white soutache 4 inches (10.2 cm) long. Use it to attach five 4-mm glass pearls at the base of the rhinestone (photo g). Add a piece of 4-inch (10.2 cm) aqua soutache. On each end of this piece, attach a 4-mm bicone (photo h). Loop the soutache around these beads, tuck the ends to the back, apply glue to them, and trim (photo i).

5 Cut a piece of white soutache 4 inches (10.2 cm) long. Use it to stitch a piece of rhinestone chain around one of the bicones. Add a piece of aqua trim, also 4 inches (10.2 cm) long. Tuck the soutache at the bottom of the beadwork to the back; loop the other loose ends to the back, with a 6-mm glass pearl inside (photo j). Repeat on the other side, mirroring the design (photo k).

e

f

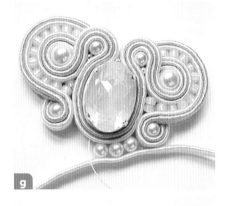

g

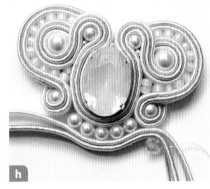

h

i

j

k

6 Cut three pieces of soutache, two white and one aqua, each 2 inches (5.1 cm) long. As shown in photo l, use them to make a bezel around the 8 x 6-mm oval rhinestone, then add an 11° seed bead to fill the gap where the braid meets. Stitch the trim together. As shown in photo m, stitch this element to the bottom of the focal element. Your element should measure approximately 2¼ x 2 inches (5.7 x 5.1 cm).

7 As shown in photo n, string on a 4-mm glass pearl, the bead cap (narrow end first), and the 17-mm polygon pendant. Stitch back through the bead cap, the glass pearl, and the soutache. Pull the thread tight. Secure the thread on the back of the bead embroidery and cut it.

Decorative Elements

8 Cut a piece of aqua soutache 4 inches (10.2 cm) long. Make a knot and secure it in the soutache, 1⅝ inches (4 cm) from one end. String on an 11° seed bead and a 6-mm glass pearl (photo o).

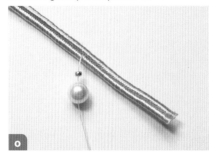

9 Wrap the soutache around the glass pearl, stitch through the trim, then pass the needle back through the glass pearl and the seed bead, as shown in photo p. (The seed bead will position itself vertically below the glass pearl.) Sew the soutache together just beyond the seed bead.

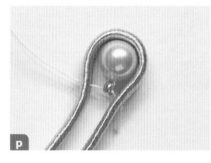

10 Cut two pieces of 4-inch (10.2 cm) white soutache and sew them around the aqua soutache, keeping your stitches tiny and invisible (photo q).

11 Attach a 4-mm glass pearl on one side of the 6-mm pearl; wrap and stitch all three pieces of braid around it (photo r). Repeat on the other side of the 6-mm pearl (photo s). Sew the ends of the soutache to the back, apply glue to the ends, and trim off any extra material.

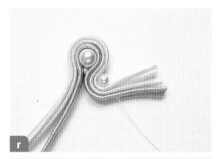

12 Cut a piece of white soutache 6 inches (15.2 cm) long. Starting from the middle of this piece, stitch it around a 4-mm pearl, adding a row of seven size 8° seed beads. (Photo t shows the beginning of this process.) With the remaining soutache and in a similar manner, stitch seven seed beads around the other 4-mm pearl.

13 Cut a piece of aqua soutache 6 inches (15.2 cm) long and stitch it to the previous row. Loop the soutache around 4-mm glass pearls on either end. Tuck the ends of the soutache to the back of the work, apply glue to them, trim, and secure (photo u).

14 Cut three pieces of soutache, two white and one aqua, each 2¾ inches (7 cm) long. Use these to make a bezel around one of the pear-shaped rhinestones (photo v), tacking the layers of trim together where they meet.

15 Cut a piece of white soutache 4 inches (10.2 cm) long. With light gray thread in your needle, use this piece to sew a piece of rhinestone chain around the bezel (photo w). Attach two more rows of soutache to this element, one white and one aqua (photo x).

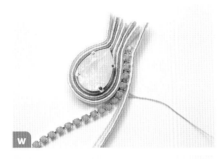

16 Attach the element finished in step 13 atop the one from step 15 as shown in photo y, passing the needle gently and carefully between the layers of soutache as you stitch.

17 As shown in photo z, bring out your thread near an 8° seed bead and string on one size 11° seed bead, one 3-mm glass pearl, one 4-mm glass pearl, one 3-mm glass pearl, and one size 11° seed bead.

18 Sew these beads above the pear-shaped rhinestone (photo aa). You've finished one decorative element (photo bb). Repeat steps 8 through 18 to make seven additional decorative elements (eight total).

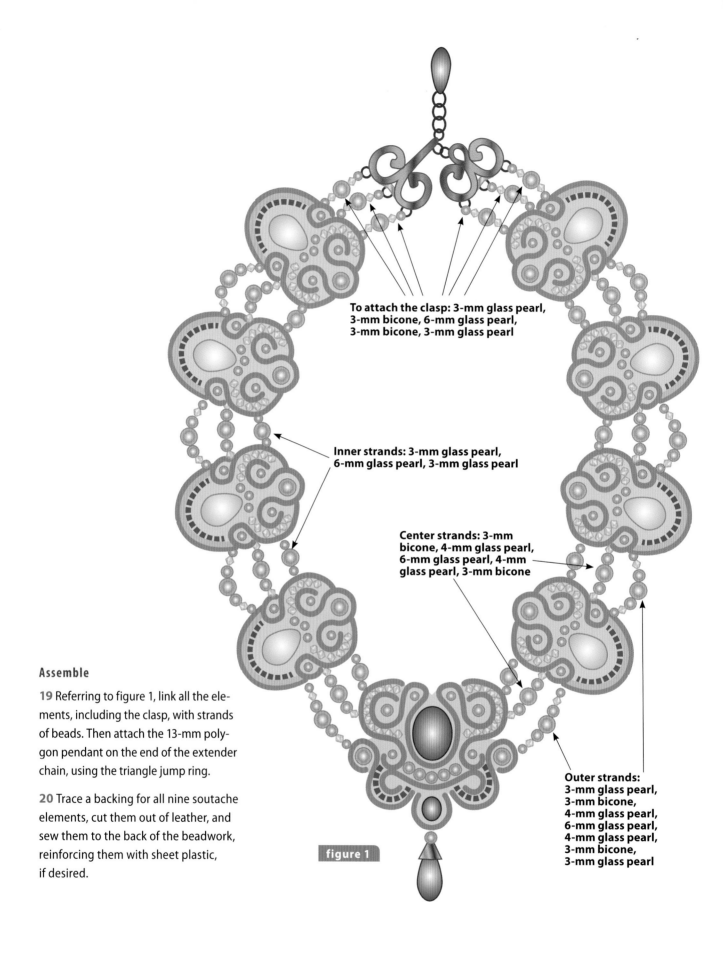

To attach the clasp: 3-mm glass pearl, 3-mm bicone, 6-mm glass pearl, 3-mm bicone, 3-mm glass pearl

Inner strands: 3-mm glass pearl, 6-mm glass pearl, 3-mm glass pearl

Center strands: 3-mm bicone, 4-mm glass pearl, 6-mm glass pearl, 4-mm glass pearl, 3-mm bicone

Outer strands: 3-mm glass pearl, 3-mm bicone, 4-mm glass pearl, 6-mm glass pearl, 4-mm glass pearl, 3-mm bicone, 3-mm glass pearl

figure 1

Assemble

19 Referring to figure 1, link all the elements, including the clasp, with strands of beads. Then attach the 13-mm polygon pendant on the end of the extender chain, using the triangle jump ring.

20 Trace a backing for all nine soutache elements, cut them out of leather, and sew them to the back of the beadwork, reinforcing them with sheet plastic, if desired.

GALLERY

1. JADWIGA BETLEY
Ombre, 2012
18.5 cm x 4 cm
Soutache, crystals, mother-of-pearl components, seed beads, silver clasp; soutache embroidery
Photo by artist

2. KAYA SOLOVIEVA
Cashmere Cream, 2012
Dimensions unknown
Soutache, seed beads, crystals, Czech glass beads
Photo by artist

3. ANNETA VALIOUS
Lilith, 2012
21 x 18 x 1 cm
Soutache, black agate, crystals, metal beads, rhinestone chain
Photo by artist

1

2

3

1. MIRIAM SHIMON
Crimson Rapture, 2012
43 x 3 x 9 cm
Soutache, seed beads, rivolis, crystals
Photo by artist

2. JADWIGA BETLEY
Rose Peach, 2012
7.5 x 4 cm
Soutache, crystals, silver
Photo by artist

3. MIRIAM SHIMON
Once Upon a Time, 2012
50 x 3 x 7 cm
Soutache, rose quartz cabochons, crystals, chatons, seed beads, rose quartz drops, rhinestones
Photo by artist

4

5

6

4. MELISSA INGRAM
Jacaranda Nights, 2011
41.5 x 8 x 1.5 cm
Soutache, crystal zipper, glass pearls, bicones, rounds,
briolette pendants, satin, column pendants, flat backs,
silver-plated crystals, crystal ring, thread
Photo by artist

5. ANNETA VALIOUS
Inconnue Pendant, 2012
10 x 7 cm
Soutache, crystals, freshwater pearls, seed beads, lace,
metal chain
Photo by artist

6. KAYA SOLOVIEVA
Boucheron, 2012
Pendant, 8 x 7 cm
Soutache, seed beads, crystals, Czech crystals, pearls
Photo by artist

1

2

3

1. ANNA SZKUDLARSKA
Malati, 2012
51 x 12 cm
Soutache, pearls, zircon, jade, crystal, silk, Czech beads, seed beads, tatting material, textiles, taffeta, leather, handmade fabric flowers; soutache embroidery, tatting
Photo by artist

2. OLGA SNETKOVA
Winter Morning, 2012
13 x 7 x 40 cm
Soutache, fluorite
Photo by artist

3. JADWIGA BETLEY
Tenderness, 2012
7.5 x 48 cm
Soutache, crystals, mother-of-pearl, seed beads
Photo by artist

5

4. ALESSANDRA DEL VITTO
Minutes to Midnight, 2012
45 x 15.5 x 0.5 cm
Soutache, crystals, hematite, seed beads;
soutache embroidery
Photo by artist

5. VERONIKA LEBEDEVA
Pink & Gray, 2011
48 x 11 cm
Soutache, japer beads, hematite beads,
pink quartz beads, cat's-eye beads,
leather; strung
Photo by artist

6. TATIANA MINKO
Mariage (Marriage), 2010
Necklace, 50 cm; bracelet, 7 x 16 cm
Soutache, rondelles, mother-of-pearl,
pearls, leather
Photo by artist

6

1. ANNETA VALIOUS
Spirit of Spring, 2012
30 x 15 x 2 cm
Soutache, nephrite, amazonite, labradorite
beads and cabochons, crystal bicones
Photo by artist

2. TATIANA MINKO
Vitrage, 2011
7 x 17 cm
Soutache, crystals, glass beads, rondelles,
bronze, leather
Photo by artist

3. ANNA SZKUDLARSKA
Peacock, 2012
14 x 5 cm
Soutache, labradorite, Czech beads, seed
beads, pearls, feathers, leather; soutache
embroidery, tatting
Photo by artist

4. KAYA SOLOVIEVA
Crystal, 2012
Dimensions unknown
Soutache, crystals, seed beads, ribbon,
silver braid, glass pearls, Czech glass beads
Photo by artist

5. ANNETA VALIOUS
Indian Inspiration Brooch, 2012
10 x 6 x 1 cm
Soutache, jasper cabochon, square beads,
magatama beads, metal beads
Photo by artist

6. ANNETA VALIOUS
Old Castle, 2012
8 x 3.5 cm
Soutache, crystals, metal beads and charms,
rhinestone chain, labradorite, seed beads, lace;
soutache embroidery
Photo by artist

Acknowledgments

I thank my family, my husband, James, and my children for the love and support they gave me as I worked on this book. They were the first to voice admiration and constructive criticism. Their advice propelled me forward and helped me to excel.

I thank my parents for everything they gave me and for the many things I learned from them. They're responsible for my appreciation for beauty, my expansive education, and this vital need I have to accomplish everything I start.

I thank my grandmother, who taught me to sew and instilled in me patience and a love for handwork.

I thank my friends for their encouragement and their empathy.

I'm grateful to Nathalie Mornu, my editor, without whom this book would never have seen the light of day—a big thank you for her enthusiasm, her support, and especially for translating my manuscript, a task that's not always so easy. Thanks, too, to Valerie Van Arsdale Shrader, Hannah Doyle, Kathleen Holmes, Ray Hemachandra, and the Lark Jewelry & Beading team members who worked on this book.

I also thank the highly talented artists who submitted imagery of their magnificent soutache jewelry for the gallery pages in this book: Melissa Ingram, Miriam Shimon, Alessandra Del Vitto, Tatiana Minko, Jadwiga Betley, Anna Szkudlarska, Olga Snetkova, Kaya Solovieva, and Veronika Lebedeva.

About the Author

Anneta Valious was born in Moscow and grew up there, the daughter of a Russian physicist. She studied psychology at the University of Moscow, but her destiny was in France, where she has lived for many years with her husband and two children.

Anneta owes her taste for beautiful things and her love of crafting to her mother and grandmother. As far back as she can remember, her mother had a passion for all things creative: music, knitting, macramé, flower arranging, and much more. When Anneta was a child, her grandmother, an outstanding seamstress and embroiderer, taught her the basics of sewing, and Anneta would stitch up custom-tailored clothes for herself, her mother, and sometimes even for friends.

Much later, in 2007, while searching for a gift for their daughter, Anneta and her husband chose a box of seed beads. That's how Anneta discovered the world of beading! For a number of months, she looked at photos of beadwork online and daydreamed—and finally she tried her own hand at it. Anneta is self-taught. She learned to beadweave and do bead embroidery from books and from the Internet. She was already familiar with jewelry made from the ornamental trims known as passementerie, having seen it exhibited in decorative arts galleries in Moscow. So it wasn't long before she began incorporating soutache into her own work. She became deeply passionate about creating her own soutache jewelry designs, and she now can't imagine life without beads.

Bead embroidery with soutache allows her to create very feminine jewelry full of graceful curves, to experiment with shapes and colors, even to dare to build up layers to make dimensional pieces. She frequently uses semiprecious gemstones and freshwater pearls. A few months after launching into jewelry fabrication, she discovered the brilliance of crystals, too.

When designing pieces, she often draws inspiration from pretty stones and color combinations. Anneta finds her muse everywhere, both in nature and in man-made things. Her favorite themes include travel, mythology, music, and space.

Credits

EDITOR AND TRANSLATOR
Nathalie Mornu

TECHNICAL EDITOR
Valerie Van Arsdale Shrader

ART DIRECTOR AND COVER DESIGNER
Kathleen Holmes

DESIGNER
Carol Morse Barnao

PROJECT PHOTOGRAPHER
Stewart O'Shields

HOW-TO PHOTOGRAPHER
Anneta Valious

ILLUSTRATORS
Page 68, J'aime Allene
All others, Melissa Grakowsky Shippee

EDITORIAL ASSISTANTS
Dawn Dillingham
Hannah Doyle

ART INTERN
Tanya Johnson

Index

AN ESSENTIAL LIBRARY OF BOOKS FOR BEADERS

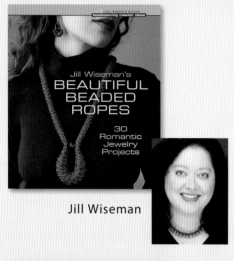

Jill Wiseman

Sabine Lippert

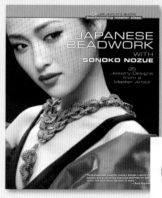

Sonoko Nozue

Sherry Serafini

Maggie Meister

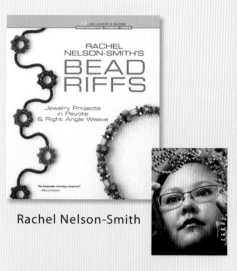

Rachel Nelson-Smith

Jamie Cloud Eakin

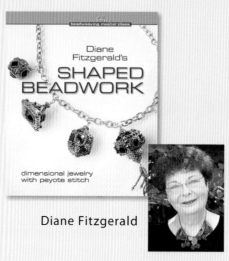

Diane Fitzgerald

Marcia DeCoster